JESUS HEALS YOU

A Proven Method to Enhance Your
Experience With Divine Healing

Dr. John Carmichael

Contents

Summary

JESUS HEALS YOU

A PROVEN METHOD TO ENHANCE YOUR EXPERIENCE WITH DI-
VINE HEALING

DR. JOHN CARMICHAEL

What if healing is not just an occasional miracle but a divine promise waiting to be unlocked? In Jesus Heals You, Dr. John Carmichael reveals a groundbreaking truth: divine healing is not random but follows a biblical pattern that anyone can apply. Through years of study, personal encounters, and miraculous testimonies, he unveils the Teach, Preach, and Heal model—a method directly drawn from the ministry of Jesus Himself.

This model was not just a theory—it was tested, and the results were astonishing. Those who immersed themselves in the biblical principles of teaching, preaching, and faith-building experienced significantly higher rates of divine healing compared to those who did not. From the supernatural survival of Dr. Carmichael's premature son to the miraculous restorations in his own body, these testimonies demonstrate the undeniable power of faith in action.

With biblical insights, real-life miracles, and practical guidance, this book is more than an exploration of healing—it's an invitation to experience it for yourself. Open these pages, apply the Teach, Preach, and Heal model, and step into the fullness of God's healing power.

Are you ready to witness the extraordinary? Healing is not just possible—it is promised.

Preface

From the beginning of time, humanity has sought healing—whether from physical ailments, emotional wounds, or spiritual burdens. While medicine and science have made tremendous advancements, there remains an undeniable need for divine healing, a touch that transcends human limitations. Jesus Heals You is a testimony to that supernatural power, a guide to understanding and experiencing the healing grace of God in your life.

This book was birthed from a personal journey of discovery. In 2006, I received a divine instruction that would change the course of my ministry: "Other than your Sunday and Wednesday sermons, I want you to study nothing but healing." At the time, I was not sick, nor did I have a personal crisis that required healing. Yet, in obedience, I immersed myself in the study of divine healing. What followed was a series of miraculous encounters—some personal, some witnessed—that deepened my faith and understanding of God's power to heal.

As I dove deeper into Scripture, I began to see healing not as an occasional miracle but as an essential part of God's plan for His people. I examined the ministry of Jesus and discovered a consistent pattern: He taught, He preached, and He healed. This divine model, recorded in Matthew 4:23 and 9:35, was not just a historical record but a blueprint for how healing is transmitted through faith.

But the real test came when my faith in healing was no longer theoretical but urgently needed. In the midst of my studies, my wife became pregnant with our fifth child. Almost immediately, complications arose. The doctors gave grim reports, predicting our son had little chance of survival. Even if he lived, they warned, he would likely suffer severe disabilities. It was then that I realized my study of healing was not an academic exercise—it was preparation for a miracle.

I applied what I had learned. I spoke God's Word over my son every day. I held fast to the Teach, Preach, and Heal model, immersing myself in the truth that faith comes by hearing the Word (Romans 10:17). As the months passed and the battle raged, we witnessed the power of divine healing firsthand. Our son, against all medical odds, survived and thrived. Today, he is perfectly healthy—a living testament to the truth that Jesus heals.

This experience, along with many others, solidified my conviction: healing is not a random occurrence but a divine provision that can be accessed through faith. However, I also realized that many believers struggle to experience this promise, not because healing is unavailable, but because the transmission of healing requires faith to be built.

This realization led me to test the Teach, Preach, and Heal model within a broader context. I began applying these principles in my ministry, encouraging others to immerse themselves in the Word, to listen to teaching and preaching on divine healing, and to activate their faith. The results were astonishing. Those who committed to studying and hearing God's promises on healing saw significant breakthroughs—many experiencing divine healing in ways they had never encountered before. Conversely, those who did not engage in this process struggled to see the same level of healing. The difference was undeniable.

Healing is more than an event—it is a process of faith, a journey of transformation that requires engagement with God's Word. This book is designed to guide you through that journey. Within these pages, you will discover:

- The biblical foundation of divine healing and its place in the atonement
- The Teach, Preach, and Heal model and how it aligns with Jesus' ministry
- Real-life testimonies of miraculous healing, demonstrating the power of faith
- Practical steps to cultivate a faith-filled environment for healing
- How to overcome doubt and strengthen your confidence in God's promises

If you have ever wondered why some receive healing while others struggle, if you have sought divine healing but felt hindered by doubt or uncertainty, this book will provide the answers and tools you need.

Healing is not reserved for a select few; it is a divine gift available to all. Whether you are seeking healing for yourself, standing in faith for a loved one, or simply desiring to deepen your understanding of God's power, this book is for you.

My prayer is that as you read, your faith will be strengthened, your hope renewed, and your body, mind, and spirit transformed by the power of God's Word. Healing is not just possible—it is promised. Step into this truth, engage with the teachings of Scripture, and witness the miraculous for yourself.

Jesus heals you. Now it's time to experience it for yourself.

~ Dr. John Carmichael

CHAPTER 1

Healing Concept

In 2006, I believe that God spoke to me these words, "Other than your Sunday and Wednesday sermons, I want you to study nothing but healing." These words were mystifying because I was not sick. Why would a healthy person be given such a strong command to study healing?

I already believed in divine healing and prayed for many people to be healed, although very few, if any, received divine healing because of my prayers. Therefore, in obedience to the divine directive, I studied divine healing. During that time, my wife, Erin became pregnant with our fifth child. Within the first month of pregnancy, dire complications arose. The baby had several health setbacks in utero and was born sixteen weeks early, weighing four-hundred and sixty grams (or just over one pound). Our son's chances of survival at that time were around ten percent. His chances of moderate to severe disability were near one hundred percent. Our son lived. He is still alive. He is perfectly healthy and functional.

Did God speak to me to prepare me to believe in divine healing? Did studying the topic of divine healing create faith for healing, as referred to in Romans 10:17? Does this scenario fit in the Christ-centered ministry model to teach, preach, and heal, as mentioned in Matthew 4:23 and 9:35? While understanding that there are several other effective Biblical approaches to divine healing, can this model, that connects teaching and preaching as a means to help people receive divine healing, be taught to people suffering so they can have an enhanced healing experience?

Personal Ministry Context and Past Experience

The theology of divine healing was not of great importance to me prior to the divine directive that occurred in January 2006. However, as mentioned, I would often pray for people to be healed. The church I began attending shortly after becoming a Christian, would pray for the sick every Sunday. They would call for the deacons and elders of the church to line up across the front of the church.

They each could have some olive oil, and the pastor would invite anyone needing prayer to come forward to receive prayer, especially if a person would need to be healed. It was just part of the culture of the church. I do not remember anyone teaching on why they included this practice in the church service. However, it made sense to be that people would receive prayer when they came to church. I was not sufficiently curious enough to ask questions or even research it myself.

Jerry B. Walker Healing Evangelist

My first experience with the healing ministry was with Evangelist Jerry B. Walker. Walker would come to the church every year. Many years before I came to the church, he had a revival in that church that lasted for weeks. Every time he came, that revival was mentioned. He was a flamboyant speaker. I had never met anyone like him. He was funny. He gave people made-up names. People came to hear him preach. In my opinion, it was the prayer lines that set him apart.

He would have the people line up around the perimeter of the sanctuary. He would them have them come to him, one by one, and he would pray for them. Some may argue that he did not really pray for them, he would touch them. He did not grab people or even lay his whole hand upon them. Just a fingertip. I would get into the prayer line. Not because was I sick, but because the presence of God was so strong in that prayer line. I have no idea whether people got healed in those lines. However, he would proclaim them healed. What was not arguable, was the sense of the presence of God in those services.

Evangelist Joe Martin

Healing evangelist Joe Martin came to our church during a 21 day fast. I was working part-time at the church. We had nightly services during the 21 days of fasting. At times, I was asked to take him to the church. On several occasions I would arrive to pick him up and he would be in a trance of some kind. One time, I had to physically move him to get him into the car. During the rides to the church, he would tell me where people would be sitting and their sicknesses. As soon as I got into the church, I would look for those people. They were sitting right where he said they would be sitting.

He would minister to them, and they would get healed. During those days, he had a special gift of healing that cured deafness. Many people would receive their hearing in those services. One time Martin ministered to a friend of mine. They had their ear drum surgically removed. God restored their hearing in that service. After that service, they went to the doctor.

The doctor refused to acknowledge the miracle by calling it "spontaneous organ regeneration." Although, I was impressed at the power of God to heal my friend's ear, I did not have the desire to pursue the healing ministry.

Personal Healing Encounters

I have had many encounters that involved dealing with divine healing. The following pages share a few of the encounters that have helped form the model that is presented in this book. God has used these healing encounters as building blocks to bring insight that is greatly needed in the discussion of divine healing.

Encounter with Ms. Hicks

The initial teaching about divine healing came very early in the conversion process. My first church experience was at Evangel World Prayer Center. As mentioned before every Sunday, the church elders were called forward, and people would come forward to be anointed with oil and receive prayer. The understanding of healing began much later.

One of the first people I prayed for as it related to healing was Ms. Hicks. Ms. Hicks was a hospital visitation pastor of EWPC. She had been diagnosed with some form of cancer some months back. She was now in the hospital as the cancer progressed. I was on staff at EWPC as a college and career pastor. Part of my duties was to visit the hospitals a couple of times a week. I visited Ms. Hicks. After my initial greeting, I asked if I could pray for her. She very sweetly accepted my invitation for prayer. My prayer went something like this, "God, if it is Your Will, please heal Ms. Hicks, but if not, we know she will be with You." She interrupted my prayer by saying, "John Carmichael, if that is the best prayer you can pray for me, please do not pray for me. If you do not already know, it is God's Will to heal, do not bother praying for me." I was thoroughly embarrassed. I asked her if I could pray for her again. She agreed. I prayed, "Ms. Hicks believes it is Your Will to heal her, so I pray that You would heal her in the Name of Jesus." Not long after that prayer meeting, she received her healing. In just a couple of weeks, she was back at her job praying for people in the hospital. She received her healing on her faith, not on my faith. At that time, I did not believe it was God's Will to heal, although no one told me to think like that.

Divine Assisted Weight-Loss

Another experience with healing came several years later when I was in my early 30s. I was about 75 pounds overweight and had some issues that correlated to being that much overweight. During a doctor's visit, the doctor asked me if I wanted to raise my children. What an odd and offensive question. Of course, I answered in the affirmative. He said, "You will not live long enough." He referred to my family history of men dying in their 30s of heart attacks and that I was gaining weight consistently. As I walked out of the doctor's office, I said, "That is his confession. God is going to keep me alive." Then I heard what I believe to be the voice of the Lord. He said, "Your faith is not strong enough to overcome your abuse to your body." I was dumbstruck. At that point, I realized I had to do something about my weight. Losing weight had been a struggle at that time in my life. I needed healing of my metabolism and a deliverance from a food addiction. For some reason, I decided to find a scripture to help with the weight loss goal.

At this point, I would meditate upon Romans 8:13. It says, ". . . for if you are living according to the flesh, you must die; but if by the Spirit you are putting to death the deeds of the body, you will live." (Rom. 8:13) Two reasons make this verse necessary in this story. First, it teaches the role humans must play to overcome flesh issues. The point is that humans will be the ones putting the flesh issues to death, but the power of the Spirit does it. Secondly, it reveals that when the Spirit overcomes flesh issues, it brings life. Life does not begin in heaven; it starts now. For a year, I confessed this verse over my body and mind.

It reminded me to depend on the Holy Spirit to help overcome food addiction. It also encouraged me to trust Him for life, not death. In about one year, I lost 75 pounds. That was many years ago; for the most part, the weight and all the issues are still gone. The power for healing and overcoming addiction had come through confession and meditation on the Word of God.

Miracle Baby

The climax and most remarkable experience is the birth of my fifth child, Joel. This experience began in January 2006. During a 21-day fast, I believe the Lord spoke to me, saying, "A change is coming to your ministry. Other than studying for the Sunday and Wednesday messages, you are to study on nothing else but healing." This was strange to me, and I had no idea what would happen. My first reaction was to reply to Him, saying, "I am not sick. Plus, I already believe in healing." In obedience to what God said, I studied the subject of healing for several months. During that time, I discovered that although I believed in healing, no one knew, if any, had received healing due to my prayers. So, because of the study of healing for several months, faith was developed. In late June of 2006, my wife became pregnant. I asked God if this was the change that was coming. He said, "The pregnancy was not the change but would coincide with the change." While that did not make much sense then, I continued to study healing. It is important to note that the previous four pregnancies were near perfect. This one started badly. About a week after discovering the pregnancy, she began to hemorrhage. Several doctors said that this would not result in a viable baby. He was born at 24 weeks weighing 460 grams (16.5 ounces). He was in the hospital for over four months. We were told on several occasions that he would not make it through the night during that time. Each day he was in the hospital, I spoke Psalm 118:17 over him. It says, "I will not die, but live, and tell of the works of the LORD." At his birth, he had less than a ten percent chance of survival and a nearly one hundred percent chance of moderate to severe disability. That was in 2006. There were nurses in the Neonatal Intensive Care Unit (NICU) who had never seen a baby that small, and that gestation age survive. If this experience had happened before the intensive study on healing, Joel would not have survived. Faith developed through the intensive study of God's Word on healing not only resulted in the survival of Joel, but he has no disabilities. Even to the point that he does not need glasses, which is unusual for babies on nearly one hundred percent oxygen for almost a year. It was a miracle.

Restored Back

A few years after that miracle of Joel, I developed severe pain in my back. For a period, I did not deal with it in any way other than taking over ten ibuprofen pills daily. This only eased the pain. My wife then convinced me to see the doctor. After they x-rayed my back, the report was terrible. He said that I had three issues with my back. He said he could fix one of them, but the other two issues he could not correct only to treat. He told me that surgery might help, but it is the kind of problem that many people must live with and manage the pain. That was not good news. At this point, I began to seek the Lord about my back. I searched the Scriptures for Bible verses on backs and bones. Every day I would spend time speaking them over my back. I would read and study healing verses from the Bible. This went on for several days. Often, I would speak the Bible verses over my back with searing pain going through my body. One day, my wife asked me if I noticed that I was not taking any more ibuprofen pills. I did not realize that I had quit taking the pills. What I noticed was that the pain was gone. The back received healing of all the issues that had previously shown up on the X-ray. This happened through using the model of teaching, preaching, and healing. Hearing and studying healing in the Bible allowed for the faith to be developed and released to receive from Jesus what He purchased because of the atonement.

Healing of Knee

In 2016, I was training for a full marathon (26.2 miles). I have run several full marathons and numerous half marathons over the years. The training went very well, with no problems. I have studied how to train safely and have done so previously with no issues. About three weeks before the race, I grew impatient with my pacing. I chose then to violate some of the rules for training by running too hard for too long, outside of routine training. After my third twenty-plus mile training run, my knee began to hurt very severely. After an examination, I discovered that I had torn my meniscus in my left knee. This type of injury will require surgery, making the race out of the question.

In prayer, I heard the Lord say, "I am going to be with you during the race." That gave me joy because I thought it would mean that God would heal my knee so I could race. However, I could not run even a mile. I did not really pray about it or deal with it in any way because of the presumption that God would heal it. So, the day of the race came. I was still in great pain. I went to the starting line in great pain, fully expecting God to heal it. As the race progressed, so did the intensity of the pain. Every mile that I ran, the pain increased, and my pace decreased. Finally, I got to the point where I would have to stop the race due to pain. I knew that at mile 10, there was a medical tent. I was going to stop at the medical tent at mile 10. I was not disappointed in God. I told the Lord that I did not understand what happened, but I was sure God was with me. Then something happened. All the pain left my knee. It was so dramatic that I thought that I had torn a nerve. I was concerned that I had lost all feeling in my left leg. Quickly I realized that I did not lose sensation in my leg. I kept running. I started to push my pace. There was no pain. I finished the rest of the race pain-free. This is not the end of the story. By the end of the night, I could not walk. I was writhing in pain. I asked God what to do. He told me, "You will walk out this miracle." I often meditated on that pun (to walk out a miracle when I could not walk). I search the Bible for verses of people getting healed in their legs and knees. I would listen to those verses and study them for several weeks every day. I would speak those verses over my knee in prayer. Although I do not know what day it happened, God supernaturally replaced the meniscus in my left knee. I still run over thirty miles a week without pain.

Each of these, except for the healing of Ms. Hicks, has two things in common. The first is the role of faith. I learned about the importance of developing and releasing faith for healing. The second is the role of Scripture in the development of faith. Faith was developed through an intensive study of God's Word about healing by reading and listening to preaching about faith. Faith for healing is more than wishing for healing. Faith for healing knows that healing is going to manifest. I developed an understanding of the difference between wanting to believe in healing and believing for healing. While wishing to receive healing, many people want to believe in healing and may erroneously even think they believe in healing. The good news is that an intensive study of the Word of God develops faith. This is at the heart of the teach, preach, and heal model of healing.

While these personal experiences are relevant to me, they pose a larger question. Can these truths be helpful to the local church just like they were to me personally? Could the challenge to study healing result in a higher confidence that healing would manifest, but something that the local church could benefit from? Is it possible that just as I thought I believed in divine healing yet did not see any healings manifest until immersed in the theology of healing, the church could see similar results?

I can verify that the answer to these questions is yes. God did not just want to do something special for one person alone. The Holy Spirit wants to use this revelation to help the local church give tools to the people in their congregations to enhance their experience with divine healing. To be sure, God desires His children to be free from the misery that results from sin. Part of the remedy could be the Holy Spirit using the teach, preach, and heal model as a way to transmit the healing that God desires for the church to receive.

Ministry Context During a Pandemic

Enhancing people's divine healing experience is especially relevant in the current today. Recently, the church has had to wrestle with COVID-19 as a global pandemic. There have been significant challenges worldwide that seem to have touched nearly every aspect of life. The church has not been immune to the ramifications of dealing with the pandemic. The church dealt with closings and changes to the formatting of church services. The mask issue was paramount in some cases. The church my wife and I pastor, did not have in-person services for two weeks and then opted for having services on the parking lot before finally having in-person services that required unique spacing in the congregation's seating and required the leaders to wear masks.

The number of COVID-19 funerals puts even more weight upon this issue of divine healing. During the pandemic, EWPC and ENC had several deaths that, according to the medical community, were directly connected to COVID-19. This has been devastating to so many families. The church could not provide the appropriate pastoral care due to not being allowed to visit the members when hospitalized. Due to the different formats caused by COVID-19, the funerals lacked the usual warmth of care that is typical and necessary. Very early in the pandemic, only a committal service took place with me as the pastor and funeral director. He held a phone while I spoke to the family via Zoom.

The Holy Spirit is challenging the church to regain its focus on bringing supernatural healing during plague-type of situations. Arguably, the church did seem to be caught off-guard in handling this pandemic. Not only from an ecclesiastical debate as to whether church services should continue during a pandemic but how the church can help those dealing with the sickness. Could or should the church be able to provide the necessary instructions to the congregants to help those who are dealing with the disease? From an eschatological perspective, it seems that plagues like COVID-19 are coming. Whether COVID-19 was what was prophesied about or not, this truth remains that plagues will be part of the last days, and the church needs to be ready to help enhance people's experience with divine healing. The model of teaching, preaching, and healing could be a tool the Holy Spirit uses in the last days.

Definition of Terms

The model of healing pursued in this book is based on nearly identical passages of Matthew 4:23 and 9:35. "Jesus was going throughout all Galilee, teaching in their synagogues and proclaiming the gospel of the kingdom, and healing every kind of disease and every kind of sickness among the people." (Matt. 4:23 NASB)[1] Mitch Curtis comments on the importance of this passage, saying, "He not only preached the kingdom of heaven; he made its presence felt in the lives of suffering humanity."[2] Charles Talbert maintains that the crowds were "attracted

---

[1]   Unless otherwise indicate all Bible references in this book are to the New American Standard Bible (NASB) (La Habra, CA: The Lockman Foundation, 1995).

[2]   Curtis Mitch and Sri Edward, *The Gospel of Matthew* (Baker Academic, 2010), 126, ProQuest Ebook Central.

to Jesus by the magnetism of his proclamation and healing."[3] Several terms from this passage will be explored, including teaching, preaching, healing, and sicknesses/diseases. Additionally, this book discusses the words "atonement" and "faith."

1. The first term is "teaching." In Greek, it is "διδάσκων." BDAG gives some basic information about this word by saying it means "to provide instruction formally and informally."[4]

2. The second term is "preaching." In Greek, it is "κηρύσσων." BDAG defines it as "proclaim aloud."[5] These first two terms are distinct because they are two different words and have somewhat different meanings. Making a clear distinction between them is difficult. The *Anchor Bible Dictionary* says that "such a sharp distinction cannot be maintained on the basis of either biblical texts or careful thought."[6] It says, "As to content, preaching without instruction lacks substance; teaching without 'kerygma' (or teaching *added*) lacks identity."[7]

NOTE: Michael Augustson defines "preaching" as "announcing the good of the Kingdom."[8] He defines "teaching" as "giving more detailed information than preaching."[9] It is my opinion that

---

3   Charles H. Talbert, *Matthew* (Baker Academic, 2010), 74–75, ProQuest Ebook Central.

4   Walter Bauer and Frederick W. Danker, "Διδάσκω," in *A Greek-English Lexicon of the New Testament and Other Early Christian Literature* (Chicago, Il: Univ. of Chicago Press, 2000), 241.

5   Bauer and Danker, "Κηρύσσω," in *A Greek-English Lexicon of the New Testament and Other Early Christian Literature*, 543.

6   Hayim Lapin, "Preaching," *Anchor Bible Dictionary*, vol. 5, ed. David Noel Freedman (New York: Doubleday, 1992), 453.

7   Lapin, "Preaching," *Anchor Bible Dictionary*, vol. 5, 453.

8   Michael Keith Augustson, "Teach, Preach, and Heal: A Series of Prescriptions for the Church on Health and Health-Care Reform," *The Covenant Quarterly* 64, no. 1–3 (February 2006): 307.

9   Augustson, "Teach," 305.

the difference between teaching and preaching is not something that be succinctly defined but subjectively discerned. I tend to like the adage that teaching is explaining and preaching is proclaiming.

3.   The third term is "healing." The *Anchor Bible Dictionary* says that in every case of healing in the Bible, "In the Greek it is "θεραπεύων.» We get the word therapy from this word. BDAG defines it as «to heal or restore."[10] The *Anchor Bible Dictionary* says that in each healing case that it is "accomplished through God's action on behalf of members of the faithful community, communicated through a human agency or by direct performance."[11] Rick Renner teaches that is word indicates a process miracle overtime, rather than an instant miracle. Many, if not most, of the miracles were over time. Therefore, θεραπεύω can certainly indicate a healing process, making it suitable for both progressive and instant healings, depending on the situation.

4.   The fourth term is "diseases." In Koine Greek, "disease" is "νόσον." BGAG defines "diseases" as "physical malady, illness."[12]

5.   The fifth term is "sicknesses." In Koine Greek, "sicknesses" is "μαλακίαν.» BGAG defines «sicknesses» as a «condition of bodily weakness."[13]

---

10   Bauer and Danker, "Θεραπεύω," in *A Greek-English Lexicon of the New Testament and Other Early Christian Literature*, 453.

11   Hayim Lapin, "Medicine and Healing," *Anchor Bible Dictionary*, vol. 4, ed. David Noel Freedman (New York: Doubleday, 1992), 664.

12   Bauer and Danker, "Νόσος," in *A Greek-English Lexicon of the New Testament and Other Early Christian Literature*, 679.

13   Bauer and Danker, "Μαλακία," in *A Greek-English Lexicon of the New Testament and Other Early Christian Literatur*, 613.

6. Another essential term in this book is "atonement." Its original meaning was "a making at one"[14] or "reconciliation," as in Romans 5:11. It is used to describe Jesus Christ's work as a priest. Atonement is the result of what happened at the death of Jesus Christ that reconciled humanity and God.[15] The *Anchor Bible Dictionary* describes atonement as "generally understood to refer to the work of Jesus in putting right the human situation in relation to God."[16] It goes on to show that atonement is defined not by one Scripture in the Bible but by a cluster of various scriptures. The *Anchor Bible Dictionary* lists four main characteristics of atonement. They are sacrifice (1 Cor. 15:3), redemption (1 Peter 1:18–19), victory over evil powers (1 Cor. 15:57), and reconciliation (Eph. 2:14–16). Some consider the atonement as a revelation of the will of God. This book assumes that when the atonement is mentioned, every aspect of the atonement is the expressed will of God.

7. Faith is a strong belief in the existence of God and confidence that He is a good Father Who gives good gifts to His children (Matt. 7:11, 1 Jn 5:14–15). Hebrews 11:6 lists these as two descriptions of faith that "please" God. The word μισθαποδότης translated as "reward," occurred only once in Hebrews as a noun and was henceforth picked up by Christian literature as a description of God.[17] The reward resulting in faith can include but is not limited to, divine healing.

---

14   Nihinlola, "By His Wounds," 20.

15   Nihinlola, "By His Wounds," 21.

16   Hayim Lapin, "Atonement," *Anchor Bible Dictionary*, vol. 1, ed. David Noel Freedman (New York: Doubleday, 1992), 518.

17   Luke Timothy Johnson, *Hebrews: A Commentary*, (Louisville: Presbyterian Publishing Corporation, 2006), 284, ProQuest Ebook Central.

These terms are tied directly to the Scripture of the proposed model. While the word atonement is not in the verses that this model of healing is founded upon, without an understanding of the atonement, any discussion of a model is futile. To be clear, if God's Will concerning healing is not known, a model to receive healing would never need to be considered. No model can overcome the Will of the Almighty.

Administering Divine Healing an Ongoing Mission

It is vital that we study divine healing because administering divine healing is an ongoing ministry of the church. Dr. Howard Ervin declares that prayer and anointing with oil for physical healing, as mentioned in James 5:14, was intended to be an ongoing ministry of the church.[18] Writing about the Great Commission (Mk. 16), Ervin points out that healing is both a "command" and a "promise" that accompanies the Great Commission.[19] In the more extended ending of the Great Commission passage in Mark 16, where Jesus says that believers "will lay hands on the sick, and they will recover." (Mk 16:15)[20] In James 5:14–15, the Scripture tells the sick person to call for the leadership of the church to anoint with oil and offer prayer with the expectation that the sick will recover. Bolstering the point that healing and preaching are part of the Gospel obligation, Trevor Grizzle, professor at Oral Roberts University, says, "Preaching and healing were interwoven and inseparable."[21] Ervin continues his point by saying that the "faith that saves is the faith that heals," meaning that healing and faith are aspects of Gospel ministry that cannot be untied.[22] Ervin declares, "The message and the signs

---

18   Howard Ervin, *Healing: Sign of the Kingdom* (Peabody: Hendrickson Publishers, 2002), 99.

19   Ervin, *Healing*, 6.

20   Stanley Horton, *What the Bible Says about the Holy Spirit* (Gospel Publishing House, Springfield, MO, 2005), 285.

21   Trevor Grizzle, *Church Aflame: An Exposition of Acts 1-12* (Cleveland, TN: Pathway Press, 2000), chap. 8, Kindle.

22   Ervin, *Healing*, 12.

were, and still are, an indivisible unity."[23] Later in this book I provide an exegesis of Romans 10:17 that demonstrates how hearing the teachings of the Bible connects to the building of faith.

23   Ervin, *Healing*, 103.

CHAPTER 2

Teach, Preach, Heal Model

Why Are Some Not Healed ?

At issue, since divine healing is part of the atoning work of Jesus and many people seek healing who do not experience healing, why are they not healed? If it were a question of God's will, if a person remains sick, it would be assumed that God did not want to heal that person. However, God wills to heal everyone, although many are not, at least on this side of heaven.

Could it be that there is a transmission problem concerning divine healing? The teach, preach, and heal model seeks to provide a possible solution to why there is a transmission problem. It has been noted by some who study healing that there are varied ways a person receives divine healing. This book presents only one of those methods of transmission of divine physical healing.

Teach, Preach, and Heal Model as a Better Model for Effective Transmission of Healing

This method of healing explores the Jesus-centered model of teaching, preaching, and healing as it relates to enhancing one's experience with divine healing. From the position of healing in the atonement, the church needs to investigate why recovery rates are low. It would make logical sense for the church to study the topic of healing to execute the will of God to His people.

Boldly, I will tell you that this model will lead to improved healing transmission. Further, building on Ervin's earlier point on the Great Commission, since healing is so intertwined with salvation as part of the Gospel obligation, does not the church have a responsibility to learn how to help people receive healing as it endeavors to help people receive salvation?

The rate of healing will dramatically increase when a person intentionally follows the Jesus model of "teach, preach, and heal." If healing is taught as an expected outcome of faith in Jesus' atonement, will there be an enhanced experience of healing? Absolutely.

The book aims to equip believers to use the Christ-centered "teach, preach, and heal" model to have an enhanced healing experience. It is my unshakable belief that if believers seeking divine healing, daily read and/or listen to sermons about divine healing will have an enhanced healing experience.

Biblical Foundation of the Teach, Preach, and Heal Model

Any model of ministry needs to be founded and built upon the solid rock of the Word of God, the Bible. Good thoughts and passionate opinions are no match for the revelation we receive from God's Word. It is ludicrous that ministerial models of any kind would be considered without a sound discussion of what the Bible says about how to minister.

Exegesis of Matthew 4:23–25 and 9:35, 38

The two nearly parallel verses are the basis of the thesis is found. I want to give more space to these verses because they connect closely to its crucial point. The nearly identical passages of Matthew 4:23–25 and 9:35, 38 provide the foundation of this Christ-centered healing model. The first verse in each of the pericopes is nearly mirrored. "Jesus was going throughout all Galilee, teaching in their synagogues and proclaiming the gospel of the kingdom, and healing every kind of disease and every kind of sickness among the people." (Matt. 4:23) Its mirrored verse is, "Jesus was going through all the cities and villages, teaching in their synagogues and proclaiming the gospel of the kingdom and healing every kind of disease and every kind of sickness." (Matt. 9:35) Scot McKnight, points out the importance of the mirroring of these verses in Matthew's writings.[24] He believes that the repetition of the three verbs (διδάσκω, κηρύσσω, and θεραπεύω) point to divisions in the Gospel and how believers should treat these verses. He writes that it is clear that Jesus' mission was three-fold. McKnight believes that the word choices of Matthew are paramount. The thrilling discovery is found in Matthew 10:1,7-8 when Jesus uses two of the three words to describe the disciples' ministry.[25] The one word that was left out was teaching. Although the disciples could not teach, by the end of the book, Jesus included teaching as part of their mission. (Matt. 28:16–20) This mission is not given to just them then but to the church today. Another observation from these pericopes would suggest that the healing would be primarily physical. This is an important distinction as this book will focus on the relationship that teaching and preaching (the method) might have on enhancing a person's experience with physical healing (the result).

---

24   Scot McKnight, "Extending Jesus," in *Devotions on the Greek New Testament: 52 Reflections to Inspire & Instruct,* ed. J. Scott Duvall and Verlyn D. Verbrugge, (Grand Rapids, MI: Zondervan, 2012), 19.

25   Duvall, *Devotions,* 20.

Information vs. Implementation of Matthew 4:23 and 9:35

Jesus Christ is not just a teacher of information, but He also teaches implementation. Alan Culpepper puts these verses in a framework that explains how they inform us about divine healing."[26] He writes that Jesus' earthly ministry was not just to provide information but to teach and to demonstrate His willingness and power to defeat every sickness and disease.[27] "Matthew presents Jesus as the Messiah and teacher to be obeyed and imitated by the church. The reader should learn from what Jesus does and what he says. The collection of miracles in Matthew 8–9 follows the teachings of Jesus in Matthew 5–7. Both serve the didactic functions of the Gospel."[28]

The importance of this idea permeates every part of this model of healing. Looking at Jesus' words and His actions as models for the church gives this model a sacredness and calling. Therefore, this model is vital, and looking at its implementation is essential. Culpepper notes that the sheer fact that these two verses nearly mirror each other makes their theme implicit in their importance.[29]

In his discussion about these two verses, he notes that in Matthew's last verses, Jesus commanded the disciples to teach everything they learned from Him.[30] Jesus' word (i.e., the power present in all his pronouncements and teachings) confirms the authority of Jesus.[31] Culpepper declares, "Jesus demonstrates the power of the kingdom both to restore and

26   Alan R. Culpepper, "Jesus as Healer in the Gospel of Matthew, Part II: Jesus as Healer in Matthew 8–9." *In Die Skriflig* 50, no. 1 (2016): 1, https://doi:10.4102/ids.v50i1. 2116.

27   Culpepper, "Jesus as Healer," 5.

28   Culpepper, "Jesus as Healer," 6.

29   Culpepper, "Jesus as Healer," 6.

30   Culpepper, "Jesus as Healer," 7.

31   Culpepper, "Jesus as Healer," 9.

forgive and to defeat the illness and turn aside the accusations of his opponents."[32]

Analysis of the Greek for the Pericopes

It is necessary to briefly look at the original language of the two texts because it will provide further evidence that the healings of Jesus were physical healings of sicknesses. Culpepper examines the phrase πᾶσαν νόσον καὶ πᾶσαν μαλακίαν, which is in both 4:24 and 9:35.[33] The term for disease, sickness, and malady is νόσος. Matthew uses the term μαλακία. None of the other Gospel writers use this word; its range of meanings is softness, delicacy, passivity, or effeminacy. βασάνος refers to pain. These definitions confirm that the healings that Jesus performed in the 4:24 and 9:35 verses are in fact healings of physical sicknesses.

Miracle Chapters

These two NT narratives are essential from a literary point of view. Jack Kingsbury notes that the Matthew 9 verse establishes what scholars have called the "miracle chapters."[34] These chapters are part of the section of Matthew where Jesus focuses on training His disciples and demonstrates the importance of implementation and demonstration of Jesus' power over sickness.[35] Kingsbury notes that the difference between 4:23 and 9:35 involves expanding Jesus' earthly ministry.[36] It is essential to realize that Jesus did not just practice this model in one place. The teaching, preaching, and healing model was characteristic of what He did everywhere He went. Nevertheless, this expansion was

---

32   Culpepper, "Jesus as Healer," 10.

33   Culpepper, "Jesus as Healer," 8.

34   Jack Dean Kingsbury,"Observations on the 'Miracle Chapters' of Matthew 8–9," *The Catholic Biblical Quarterly* 40, no. 4 (October 1978): 559.

35   Kingsbury, "Observations," 562.

36   Kingsbury, "Observations," 566.

not just geographical. He multiplies Himself through His disciples. Kingsbury writes, "As for Jesus' ministry of healing, this is described in chapters 8 and 9. But in this, too, the disciples, empowered by Him (10:1), participate, so that both He and they are said to "heal every disease and every infirmity."[37] It is logical to believe that the disciples would emulate the same transmission model of healing by including faith-building teaching and preaching.

These two verses concern the discipleship level of those who would hear the teaching and preaching as they received divine healing. Talbert gives two strands of evidence that support the state of the commitment of those healed.[38] First, the context of the Scripture demonstrates their continued discipleship. In 5:1– 2, Matthew writes that Jesus's disciples come to Him, and he teaches them. In Matthew 7:28, the crowds are astonished by the teaching of Jesus.

He says these two texts make one believe that the sermon targeted the disciples. Secondly, in a macro-Gospel context, it can be concluded that those healed were followers of Jesus, not just those who showed up for a one-time experience. He says, "The verb ἀκολουθεῖν (to follow) in Matthew means in both a strictly literal sense of 'coming or going after a person' and in a metaphorical/theological sense of discipleship. The crowds in Matthew can sometimes be regarded as Jesus's disciples."[39] This further establishes that they were in a steady state of hearing the teaching and preaching of Jesus. The people were continually encouraged and taught to believe in Jesus and obtain healing as a Kingdom dynamic. He concludes a discussion on these verses by noting that Jesus

---

37   Kingsbury, "Observations," 566.
38   Talbert, *Matthew*, 73.
39   Talbert, *Matthew*, 74.

"gave them (the disciples) authority to cast out unclean spirits and to heal every disease and illness."[40]

These two Matthew verses help establish the thesis. They provide the scope of Jesus' teaching as providing information and implementation of the Kingdom of God, which includes divine healing. They also show that Jesus did not just do this model once, but everywhere He went. Additionally, He sent His disciples to duplicate what He did. These verses demonstrate the state of those receiving healing as being present regularly in Jesus' teaching and preaching sessions.

Teaching and Preaching as a Model for Transmission of Healing

To not be redundant, but we need to see that teaching, preaching, and healing is an aspect of Jesus as a model for transmitting healing. They are not three disconnected activities but rather they are intertwined. There is a Biblical justification for using this as a model. I will point out that preaching affects faith which can enhance a person's experience with divine healing. This model is being used to bring healing in various forms.

Biblical Foundation of Teach, Preach, and Healing Model

The model the project will examine is based on two very similar scriptures in Matthew. The first is Matthew 4:23, "Jesus was going throughout all Galilee, teaching in their synagogues and proclaiming the gospel of the kingdom, and healing every kind of disease and every kind of sickness among the people." The second is Matthew 9:35, "Jesus was going through all the cities and villages, teaching in their

---

40   Talbert, *Matthew*, 131.

synagogues and proclaiming the gospel of the kingdom, and healing every kind of disease and every kind of sickness." According to Mitch Curtis' commentary on Matthew, this was very important.

He writes, "He not only preached the kingdom of heaven; he made its presence felt in the lives of suffering humanity."[41] Jesus did not just give theory; He gave them experience. In his commentary on Matthew, Charles Talbert writes that the crowds were "attracted to Jesus by the magnetism of his proclamation and healing."[42] There is a connection between the teaching/preaching and the healing ministry of Jesus. The inspired writer Matthew wrote those two verses so similarly that it appears to be a pattern. Using "all" as a reference to the various places He visited makes it seem like these were His activities everywhere He went. Jesus is the model for Christian living. His ways of ministering should be a model, as well.

Hear and Be Healed

On the other side of the miracle we experienced, we had a question. Was this a one-off miracle or was this some ancient truth that can be repeated? Could this be used again by others in order for them to experience divine healing in their life?

This book will explore those questions. In preceding pages of this book, you will discover the results of this truth as it has been examined. The results are amazing. However, do not gloss over them. What has been done here needs to continue to be examined. More importantly, the church needs to thank God that He has given us a way to connect to His healing power. As you read this book, you will find yourself going

41 Mitch and Edward, *The Gospel of Matthew*, 126.
42 Talbert, *Matthew*, 131.

in and out of the healing study. We will examine many different aspects of the healing ministry, especially as it relates to the overall truths that hearing the Word preached will help you connect to the healing power of God that was purchased in the atonement of Jesus Christ.

God's Prescription for Healing

The scriptures clearly outline a divine prescription for healing: hearing the Word of God. This principle is deeply rooted in both Old and New Testament teachings. Just as a doctor provides a prescription for medicine with specific instructions on dosage and timing, God has given us a spiritual prescription through His Word:

"My son, give attention to my words; Incline your ear to my sayings. Do not let them depart from your sight; Keep them in the midst of your heart. For they are life to those who find them And health to all their body." (Proverbs 4:20-22, NASB)

When we prioritize listening to and meditating on God's Word, healing begins to manifest in our lives. The psalmist echoes this truth: "He sent His word and healed them, And delivered them from their destructions." (Psalm 107:20, NASB) The Word of God is more than a set of written instructions; it is alive and active, full of power to bring transformation and restoration. To embrace this prescription fully, we must engage with the Word in multiple dimensions:

Listening with Intention

Just as Jesus frequently instructed His followers, "He who has ears to hear, let him hear," listening with intention requires more than passive reception. It demands an active posture of focus and readiness to obey.

Through careful and thoughtful listening, we position ourselves to receive the healing that flows from the truth.

Meditating on the Word

Meditation on scripture allows the Word to sink deeply into our hearts. This process involves reading, reflecting, and praying over the truths of God, enabling His promises to renew our minds and shape our perspective. As Proverbs 4:21 says, "Do not let them depart from your sight; keep them in the midst of your heart."

Speaking the Word in Faith

Declaring God's promises activates faith. When we speak the Word aloud, we affirm its truth and align our hearts with God's power. Confession plays a vital role in applying the healing prescription. For instance, declaring, "By His stripes, I am healed" (Isaiah 53:5) strengthens our faith and reinforces the healing process.

Trusting the Process

Healing often involves trusting God's timing and methods. Just as a patient follows a doctor's regimen without immediate results, believers must trust that God's Word is at work even when the evidence is not immediately visible. Psalm 107:20 assures us of the Word's power to heal and deliver: "He sent His word and healed them."

This prescription for healing is not a quick fix but a transformative journey that builds our faith, renews our spirit, and restores our bodies. As we delve into the remaining sections of this chapter, we will further explore how hearing the Word positions us to receive the fullness of healing Jesus has purchased for us.

The Pattern of Healing Ministry

Throughout the earthly ministry of Jesus Christ, a consistent and intentional pattern of healing ministry emerges: **proclamation of the Word, teaching of the Kingdom, and miraculous healings**. This divine sequence demonstrates that healing is inseparably tied to the Word of God.

Jesus' Ministry Blueprint

The Gospels provide numerous accounts of Jesus' ministry. A clear example is found in Matthew's Gospel: *"Jesus was going throughout all Galilee, teaching in their synagogues and proclaiming the gospel of the kingdom, and healing every disease and every sickness among the people."* (Matthew 4:23, NASB)

This pattern of teaching, proclaiming, and healing is not merely descriptive but prescriptive for the Church today. Jesus' actions reveal that hearing the Word precedes faith, and faith activates the miraculous. Healing is not an isolated act but a part of the holistic Kingdom message.

Jesus' ministry is timeless. There are no better ideas of ministry that the one that Jesus gives. It supersedes time. It continues through ever societal shift. It matches each generation right where they are. Jesus' ministry is both immanent and transcendent all at the same time. The model of teaching, preaching, and healing worked for them then. It works for us now.

Historical Continuation of the Pattern

From the early Church to modern-day revivals, this pattern has persisted. In the Acts of the Apostles, Peter and John exemplify this continuity: *"But Peter said, 'I do not have silver and gold, but what I do have I give to you: In the name of Jesus Christ the Nazarene, walk!' And grasping him by the right hand, he raised him up; and immediately his feet and his ankles were strengthened."* (Acts 3:6-7, NASB) The apostles followed the same steps—proclaiming the Word, building faith, and invoking the name of Jesus for healing. These acts affirmed the Kingdom's presence and power among God's people.

Modern-Day Witnesses

The healing ministry continues through contemporary witnesses who have embraced the biblical pattern. Evangelists such as Maria Woodworth-Etter and Smith Wigglesworth carried the torch, demonstrating that faith-filled preaching and hearing the Word are precursors to healing miracles. Their ministries mirrored the example set by Jesus and the apostles, showing that the healing power of God is timeless and available to all who believe.

Hearing as the Key to the Pattern

A foundational aspect of this pattern is the act of hearing: *"Faith comes from hearing, and hearing by the word of Christ."* (Romans 10:17, NASB) Without hearing the Word, faith cannot arise. This principle underscores the necessity of preaching and teaching within the healing ministry. Those who receive the Word with open hearts position themselves for divine intervention.

Submission to God's Order

To experience the fullness of God's healing power, believers must submit to this divine order. Healing flows through adherence to the pattern Jesus established. By prioritizing hearing, aligning with the truth of the Word, and stepping out in faith, we participate in the supernatural work God desires to accomplish in our lives.

This pattern of healing ministry, rooted in Scripture and confirmed by history, continues to demonstrate God's unchanging desire to heal and restore His people. This connection between hearing and healing underscores a divine principle: **the Word of God is the seed of healing.**

The Priority of Hearing

Hearing holds a central place in God's plan for His people. It is through hearing the Word of God that faith is birthed, sustained, and activated. Jesus emphasized this truth repeatedly during His ministry: *"Take care what you listen to. By your standard of measure it will be measured to you; and more will be given you besides."* (Mark 4:24, NASB)

Hearing Shapes Faith

Faith begins where the will of God is known, and hearing the Word reveals His will for our lives. Romans 10:17 affirms this principle: *"Faith comes from hearing, and hearing by the word of Christ."* Without a clear understanding of the Word, faith remains dormant. Hearing God's promises and truths awakens the potential for healing, restoration, and transformation.

Focused and Intentional Listening

In a world filled with competing voices, focused and intentional listening is critical. Much like tuning a radio to the correct frequency, believers must actively filter out distractions and align themselves with God's voice. This requires:

Prioritizing Time: Setting aside regular time to hear the Word, whether through scripture reading, sermons, or worship.

Eliminating Distractions: Removing sources of noise and confusion that hinder spiritual focus.

Cultivating a Receptive Heart: Approaching the Word with humility and openness to receive its truths.

The Power of Repetition

Repetition reinforces truth. Hearing the Word repeatedly strengthens faith and solidifies God's promises in our hearts. This is why scripture encourages continual meditation on the Word. Joshua 1:8 declares: "This Book of the Law shall not depart from your mouth, but you shall meditate on it day and night." To meditate on the Word would mean that each person would speak the Word of God over and over to themselves. Notice here that Joshua's success and prosperity was dependent upon his relationship with the Word. God wanted success and prosperity for Joshua. However, it was not just going to happen because God wanted it for him. Joshua had to obey the commandment to stay in relationship with God's Word for him to walk in that success and prosperity. It absolutely follows the model of ministry that would ask people to stay with action of receiving the Word of God to enhance their experience with divine healing.

Hearing Produces Action

True hearing leads to action. James 1:22 exhorts us: "But prove yourselves doers of the word, and not just hearers who deceive themselves." Hearing without obedience renders the Word ineffective. When we act on what we hear, we activate the transformative power of God in our lives.

Hearing and Healing

The connection between hearing and healing is vividly illustrated in the Gospels. In Luke 5:15, crowds gathered to hear Jesus and to be healed. This pattern underscores that hearing precedes healing; the Word creates an atmosphere where faith can flourish, making miracles possible.

Hearing is not passive; it is an active engagement with God's truth. By prioritizing hearing, believers position themselves to receive the fullness of God's promises, including healing, peace, and abundant life.

Hearing Leads to Faith and Healing

Consider the example of the lame man at Lystra:

"At Lystra a man was sitting who had no strength in his feet, lame from his mother's womb, who had never walked. This man was listening to Paul as he spoke, who, when he had fixed his gaze on him and had seen that he had faith to be made well, said with a loud voice, 'Stand upright on your feet.' And he leaped up and began to walk." (Acts 14:8-10, NASB)

Three principles emerge from this narrative:

1. **He Followed the Prescription:** The man was listening attentively.

2. **He Submitted to the Pattern:** His faith grew as he heard the Word, and healing followed.

3. **He Overcame Challenges:** Despite being lame, he prioritized hearing, demonstrating the effort it took to position himself where the Word was being proclaimed.

Aligning with God's Healing Plan

To receive the healing Jesus purchased, we must:

1. **Read, hear, and meditate** on God's Word.

2. **Obey and believe** the truths revealed.

3. **Understand** that the Word is working healing within us, even when it is not immediately visible.

Jesus' ministry provides a clear example for us to follow. As the psalmist reminds us:

"He sent His word and healed them." (Psalm 107:20, NASB)

Let us commit to spending time in the Word, allowing it to transform our thinking, renew our faith, and bring healing to every area of our lives.

CHAPTER 3

Healing in the Atonement

"That white preacher just changed my theology." The pastor at a primarily African-American church said those words to me. I was asked to preach at the church. It was amazing. I was so excited. It is always a joy to preach in a church that "talks back" to you while you are preaching. This was one of those exciting churches. Knowing this about the congregation, I prepared a "hot" sermon. I knew it would set the church on fire. I could not wait. When I woke up the morning of the service, God spoke to me. He told me to preach a message called the "The Double Cure." I was not happy about with what He said. I made deals with Him. I begged Him to change His mind. I convinced myself that I was engaging on some self-sabotage mission and it was not God speaking. However, the more I resisted, the stronger it came. What did I do? I brought both messages. Maybe God would see if I would be willing to preach "The Double Cure" and then allow for my "hot" message. He did not relent.

What is the "The Double Cure"? It is a message tracing the mentioning of forgiveness of sins to the healing of sicknesses. It starts with the famous passage of Isaiah 53 (which will be exegeted later). Then it proceeds to Psalm 103, where David praises God for forgiving all his sins and healing all his diseases. The message highlights the time Jesus asked which would be easier, to forgive sins or to heal sicknesses.

It concludes with the passage of James which connects that after the anointing of oil and the prayer of faith the sick person would be made well and if they have committed any sin it would be forgiven. There will be more on those items later.

The message, The Double Cure, was preached. It was well received. People who needed healing were asked to come forward. Each one was anointed with oil and the prayer of faith was released.

A general Bishop was there in attendance that day. His denomination did not believe in divine healing. The pastor of the church did not know the Bishop was coming that day. The pastor told me that when I started preaching, he started sweating.

The Bishop came for prayer. He had just be diagnosed with cancer. I prayed for him, however, I did not know anything about him. I just prayed in faith.

After the service, as was the custom of that church, I was escorted to the pastor's office. The pastor came into the office an a sort of panic and excitement. He told me about the Bishop. He told me what the Bishop said. Evidently, the sermon, was enough to get him to believe that just as God wants to forgive sin, He wants to heal sickness. It changed his theology.

A few weeks later, the pastor called. The Bishop was healed.

The theological framework of "The Double Cure" is better known as healing in the atonement. It is the foundation of any expectation of healing. Without an understanding of the healing in the atonement doctrine, any model of healing is meaningless and completely void of a reason to believe in consistent healing. Healing would be based upon various and changing aspects that would make it so subjective that one could hardly have faith for healing.

Healing in the Atonement

The healing methodology presented in this book is from a doctrinal position that healing is part of Jesus Christ's atonement. Roots of the healing in the atonement doctrine have been traced to Europe, where Presbyterian Edward Irving (1830), Lutheran Johann Blumhardt (1843), Dorothea Trudel (1851), and Otto Stockmayer (1867) taught that healing in the atonement was appropriated by prayer.[43] Stockmayer's Sickness and the Gospel is credited to have pioneered the idea that physical healing was part of the atonement.

This doctrine is essential as it casts a shadow on every aspect of this book. Periodically, sections throughout this book address this topic. William Menzies, writing on the fundamental beliefs of the Assemblies of God, explains the doctrinal position of healing in the atonement.[44] The doctrine avers that sickness and death came because of the original sin of the first couple.[45]

The atonement not only dealt with the curse of sin but, as a result, brought about the potential of healing sickness. The atonement removes the cause of physical sickness, original sin, and therefore it removes the consequence, sickness.[46]

---

43   Vinson Synan, "A Healer in the House? A Historical Perspective on Healing in the Pentecostal/Charismatic Tradition," *Asian Journal of Pentecostal Studies* 3, no. 2 (July 2000), 191.

44   Stanley Horton, William W. Menzies, *Bible Doctrines: A Pentecostal Perspective* (Logion Press, 2015), 195.

45   Horton, Menzies, *Bible Doctrines*, 191.

46   Horton, Menzies, *Bible Doctrines*, 195–196.

Healing of Sickness and Forgiveness of Sin

The healing in the atonement doctrine requires some clarification since the atonement relates to the healing of sickness and the forgiveness of sin. The doctrine of healing in the atonement does not assume that disease is a sin.[47] The disease is a consequence of original sin. Disease does not interfere with humanity's relationship with God. Sin does. Sin and sickness are in different categories, and the atonement affects them differently. Forgiveness of sin is a permanent state, whereas healing is not.[48] The nature of healing in the atonement doctrine is multi-dimensional. Salvation and healing differ in structure even though they were dealt with because of the suffering, resurrection, and ascension of Jesus Christ.

Martin Luther describes the multidimensional aspect of the atonement.[49] He explains that just as a person is forgiven, it does not always mean they cease to be sinners in the same way a person will be healed, but that does not always mean they are free from illness. He continues that this is similar to a person being declared righteous by God because of the atonement yet still deals with sin and will deal with sin until death. Likewise, a person will be healed by faith in the atonement yet deal with sickness until death. The person who has faith in Jesus is forgiven, even though they continually deal with sin throughout life. The person who has placed faith in Jesus is healed even though they deal with sickness and could potentially die due to sickness. Forgiveness is instant and permanent. Sanctification, as described as becoming more like Jesus, is progressive. Healing is instantly available and can manifest instantly or

---

47   Bruce R. Reichenbach, "Healing View," in *The Nature of the Atonement: Four Views. Spectrum Multiview Book Series*, ed. James K. Beilby and Paul R. Eddy, (Downers Grove, IL: IVP Academic, 2006), 139.

48   Reichenbach, "Healing View," 140.

49   Reichenbach, "Healing View," 140.

progressively. While waiting for the coming of Jesus Christ, healing is always temporary, as a person will die of something.

There are similarities and differences, like the healing in the atonement as it relates to sickness and sin. Through understanding these points, a sick person should never be victimized, as some of the opponents of the healing in the atonement doctrine suggest is inevitable.[50] The healing in the atonement doctrine does not assume that a person suffering or dying from an illness is somehow not spiritually saved or deficient. The atonement is a revelation of God's will to banish sin and all its results from humanity. Humanity will experience varied results on this side of heaven but will experience all the blessed results in eternal life.

The Problem with Healing in the Atonement

The doctrine of healing in the atonement, as a revelation of God's will concerning the healing of sickness, does bring up a problem. The Bible is filled with stories of supernatural healing. Ronald Kydd writes that "divine healing is an ongoing phenomenon."[51] Early Christian historian Adolf von Harnack writes that Christianity has always assumed the "form of the religion of salvation and healing."[52] However, the problem is that today, some perceive the number of people experiencing healing to be less than what is recorded in Biblical history. Chittaranjan Andrade, professor of Psychopharmacology, and Rajiv Radhakrishnan, research officer, offer some staggering statistics concerning prayer for healing. In several triple-blind studies, they wrote from a statistical analysis that

---

50   Randall Holm, "Healing in Search of Atonement: With a Little Help from James K.A. Smith," *Journal of Pentecostal Theology* 23, no. 1 (2014): 50. doi:10.1163/17455251-02301007.

51   Ronald Kydd, *Healing through the Centuries: Models for Understanding* (Peabody, MA:Hendrickson, 1998), xxi.

52   Adolf von Harnack, *The Mission and Expansion of Christianity in the First Three Centuries* (Grand Rapids, MI: Christian Classics Ethereal Library, 1908), 97.

prayer had little positive effect on recovery rates for those seeking healing in areas of heart disease and diabetes. One study they examined found that adverse outcomes and complications for those recovering from surgery were higher for those receiving prayer. Only one study showed prayer having positive results, which was in the case of success rates of in vitro fertilization.[53]

Kydd records some rather sobering statistics. For instance, he writes that Oral Roberts said, ". . . he would be the happiest man on earth if he could bring healing to a quarter of the people who wanted it."[54] Peter Wagner's self-reporting system stated that 29 percent of the people were healed.[55] Kydd concludes that while even those numbers are low, there is significant evidence that healings did occur.[56] These studies and statistics seem to fall short of Matthew 4:24, where all who came to Jesus were healed.

The belief that physical healing is in the atonement makes this an issue that should be addressed. From a theological point of view, Emiola Nihinlola, a Ugandan theologian and pastor, examined the topic of healing in the atonement. Nihinlola concludes that healing provided by atonement includes physical, mental, and spiritual.[57] Nihinlola writes that sicknesses and diseases are products of sin that ultimately resulted from Adam's original sin.[58] Jesus had compassion for those suffering from all kinds of sickness and gave His life (atonement) so that they could experience healing, including physical healing.

---

53   Chittaranjan Andrade, and Radhakrishnan Rajiv, "Prayer and Healing: A Medical and Scientific Perspective on Randomized Controlled Trials," *Indian Journal of Psychiatry* 51, no. 4 (2009): 249.

54   Kydd, *Healing through the Centuries*, xxii.

55   Kydd, *Healing through the Centuries*, xxii.

56   Kydd, *Healing through the Centuries*, xxii.

57 Emiola Nihinlola, "'By His Wounds We Are Healed'; A Theological Examination of the Nature of Healing in the Atonement," *Ogbomosa Journal of Theology* XVII (2013): 23.

58   Nihinlola, "By His Wounds," 22.

The Atonement Makes Healing Available

The doctrine of healing in the atonement reveals that the causation of sickness is sin; the cure for sin is in the atonement (the death, burial, and resurrection of Jesus Christ); therefore, healing would be potentially available to every believer in Jesus Christ. To help bring definition, Lapin's *Anchor Bible Dictionary* provides a definition of "atonement." The ABD defines atonement as "generally understood to refer to the work of Jesus in putting right the human situation in relation to God."[59] Hayim Lapin's contribution to the ABD refers to several themes and supporting scriptures to describe atonement. They are sacrifice (1 Cor. 15:3), redemption (1 Peter 1:18–19), victory over evil powers (1 Cor. 15:57), and reconciliation (Eph. 2:14–16). These themes and scriptures serve as the bedrock foundation for healing in the atonement argument that speaks to the availability of healing and the revelation that healing is God's will because it has been made available through the atonement.

Causation of Sickness

Within the topic of atonement, the discussion typically concentrates on two issues. The first issue is the causation of sickness. Many theologians very succinctly identify sickness as being caused by sin. This is important to the overall premise of this book because one can readily find the cure or discern the cure due to the identification of the causation of sickness. In his book, Newman Hall provides an exhaustive examination of atonement. The book examines atonement from a microscopic to a macroscopic view. Hall writes, "He did suffer on our behalf the many consequences of sin – physical infirmities, social wrongs, the malignity of the wicked, and anguish."[60]

---

59   Lapin, "Atonement," Anchor Bible Dictionary, vol. 1, 518.

60   Newman Hall, Atonement: The Fundamental Fact of Christianity (New York: F. H. Revell, 1893), 88.

Historian and professor Amanda Porterfield has noted that healing is a fundamental experience of Christianity. She found that healing was so extensive in the history of the Church that she felt it needed a focus. She identified that the "causal effects of sin and evil are a sickness."[61] She mentions that there are various ways of healing. This is important to this project because it examines the Christ-centered model of the transmission where He would teach, preach, and heal.

Nihinlola's study of healing in the atonement has provides a vital observation.[62] One overall point of the journal article is that there was no sickness before the fall of humanity. Nihinlola pulls on the creation story to expose where sickness originated.

Father Richard Jones, director of the Spiritual Care Department at Mercy Hospital, writes about healing from a Catholic perspective and his ministry experience. Jones writes, "Because of sin, sickness, and death have entered the world, but the resurrection of Jesus overcame them, who hears the cries of those in need, healing the sick and raising the dead to life."[63]

These theologians connect sickness to original sin. Note: this doctrine is focused on original sin as opposed to individual sin. Understanding healing in the atonement leads to the next point, which is the cure.

Atonement Removed The Consequence Of Sin

The second issue of atonement is the removal of the cause. We identify atonement as the agent that removes the consequences of sin.

---

61   Amanda Porterfield, Healing in the History of Christianity (Oxford: Oxford Press, 2005), 5.

62   Nihinlola, "By His Wounds," 20.

63   Richard Jones, "The Healing Power of Christ: Scripture Shows the Importance of Faith to Those Who Are Ill," The Priest 75, no. 2 (Feb 2019): 40.

Howard Ervin argues that the three-fold ministry of Jesus to teach, preach, and heal manifests Jesus' power over Satan and asserts God's reign.[64] The atonement that Jesus provided confronts sickness resulting from the first couple's sin due to the temptation of Satan.

Nihinlola explains extensively that the death, burial, and resurrection of Jesus removed the consequences of sin, opening the way for Divine healing of sickness.[65] Randall Holm affirms this point when he writes, "Disease and suffering were tagged as consequences of the Fall and in need of redemption not unlike the soul."[66]

The point is that the atonement redeems the soul from the effects of the Fall. The same atonement redeems the physical part of humanity. The removal of the cause of sickness for humanity makes it available for the removal of sickness for humankind.

The Healing Ministry of Jesus – Permanent or Temporary

The assumption that divine healing is one of the benefits of the atonement and not just part of Jesus' earthly ministry or a temporary dispensational phenomenon provides the basis for this model of divine healing. The teaching that healing is part of the atonement has been predominately part of the Pentecostal doctrine.[67] Jesus' primary goal was to heal physical bodies and every aspect of a person.[68] Not to contradict the previous statement, Deborah Schmid points out that the Scripture's use of the word "healing" is physical[69] and should be treated

---

64   Ervin, Healing, 1.

65   Nihinlola, "By His Wounds", 23.

66   Holm, "Healing," 2.

67   Kydd, Healing through the Centuries, 201.

68   Nihinlola, "By His Wounds," 24.

69   Deborah Schmid, "Healing in the Atonement of Isaiah 52:13–53:6" (Masters Thesis, Oral

as meaning to be cured of the disease.[70] Schmid's point counters the idea that healing, as spoken of in these verses, excludes physical healing, as some may want to only focus on the spiritual healing aspect of the atonement. This understanding of healing as part of the atonement undergirds the thesis because one can expect healing in the same way one can expect the new birth.

Parameters of Divine Healing

We maintain that there are some parameters of divine healing. One of those parameters is the scope of healing in that it affects the whole person. Then there is the parameter of the connection of healing being faith. As well as the parameter of the spectrum of time in the "now" and the "not yet" aspect of the Kingdom.

Whole Person Healing

It is a fact that Biblical healing pertains to the whole person. One might say that Ervin's book is filled with the mindset that healing includes the entirety of what a human is. There is the healing of the spirit, soul, and body. Paul wrote in 1 Thessalonians 5:23 when he teaches that God is at work in a person's "spirit and soul and body." Beyond the individual, there is a healing of relationships and cultural healing. Hall writes that the atonement did not just change the character of humanity but also the condition of humanity.[71] He concludes that a surrendered person will surely experience a change in character. Stanley Burgess points out that Pentecostal and Charismatic movements emphasize the presence and the power of the Holy Spirit. He identifies an overarching mission

Roberts University, Tulsa, OK, 2013), 77, ProQuest Dissertations & Theses Global.

70   Schmid, "Healing In The Atonement," 78.

71   Hall, Atonement, 15.

49

that the Pentecostal/Charismatic movement has as being agents of healing the whole person.[72]

Nevertheless, the effect of the atonement is not limited to the inner person alone but also manifests in the outer person. The atonement affects the entire person. This would remove the limitation that a surrendered person should only expect that faith in the atonement will only have benefits on the other side of eternity. There is no compartmentalization with the work of the Spirit in a person's life. One can expect that if there is a sickness in any area, God wants to heal it.

Now and Not Yet Aspects of Healing

The "now" and "not yet" aspects of human interaction with the Kingdom of God are fundamental to the topic of healing. Experientially we see that not everyone who is seemingly asking in faith for divine physical healing sees its manifestation on this side of heaven. Ronald Kydd writes that only "2 or 3 percent of those for whom Oral Roberts prayed for was healed instantly . . ."[73] David Harrell points out that Oral said that "person after person came by with apparently no miraculous results."[74] Roberts told a reporter in 1955 that he would be the "happiest man in the world" if he "could bring healing to 25 percent of those who ask for it."[75] Kydd continues to quote various other healing ministers' statistics. His point does not dispute the availability of divine healing but only points out that it seems that right now, the church is seeing

---

72   Stanley Burgess, Encyclopedia of Pentecostal and Charismatic Christianity (New York: Taylor & Francis Group, 2006), 5.

73   Kydd, Healing through the Centuries, xxii.

74   David Edwin Harrell, Jr., Oral Roberts: An American Life (Bloomington: Indiana University Press, 1985), 456.

75   Phil Dessauer, "God Heals, I Don't," Coronet Magazine (October 1955): 57.

only a small percentage compared with the Biblical record. He teaches that one must accept the "idea of mystery"[76]

concerning divine healing and the atonement. Humans cannot expect to have everything figured out. There are so many things that one cannot know. Kydd says, "There are no formulas to assure that a miraculous cure will take place; there is no foolproof ritual or perfect place."[77] To offer a word of confirmation, Ghanaian pastor Opoku Onylnah writes, "everyone needs to exercise faith in the healing power of Jesus with the understanding that we are in between now and not yet."[78]

He maintains that this pastoral approach will help to provide a more balanced view of healing. It also helps those who have not experienced healing themselves, to keep their faith in Jesus Christ. When this truth is not applied, it creates an environment for faulty conclusions.

Conclusion of Parameters of Healing

These healing parameters will prove the most useful in the book's position that studying divine healing will enhance your experience with divine healing. At the same time, the project's focus is physical healing and understanding that healing affects the whole person will allow for tools that might be limited to the inner person to facilitate healing in the outer person. It is vital for the infirm person seeking divine healing to recognize the relationship between healing and faith.

One must realize that following a formula without mixing it with faith does not often produce healing from the Biblical record. Faith also

---

76   Kydd, Healing through the Centuries, 215.

77   Kydd, Healing through the Centuries, 215.

78   Opoku Onylnah, "God's Grace, Healing, and Suffering," International Review of Mission 95, no. 377 (January 4, 2006): 126.

should not be used to harm people who did not receive their healing manifestation on this side of eternity. The literature also provides the understanding that healing, as with any other part of the Kingdom, has aspects that a believer can expect now and will experience the miracle later the other side of eternity of heaven.

CHAPTER 4

Faith and Healing

One of the more controversial subjects of healing involves the role of faith. Faith's role in healing has led to abuse of the afflicted. Jennifer Cox suggests that the belief that faith has a role in healing has caused people with disabilities to shun the church due to persecution by those who insist on them believing for healing.[79]

This is why this subject will be approached from a sensitivity based upon awareness of abuse while attempting to acknowledge the challenging words concerning faith and healing. Faith for healing by a sick person is present in many healing narratives. Scripture also describes occasions where healing occurs when faith is lacking or not mentioned.

To further complicate the matter, there is an occasion where the limitation of Jesus' miracle ministry resulted from a lack of faith, called unbelief. The role of faith and healing has some mystery to it.

---

79   Jennifer Cox, "A Re-Examination of Faith and Healing in the Gospels: Toward a Pentecostal Theology of Healing and Disability," Cyberjournal for Pentecostal-Charismatic Research 24 (June 2017): http://www.pctii.org.oralroberts.idm. oclc.org/cyberj/cyberj24/cox.html.

Faith Present in Healing Narratives

Faith often played a role in the healing narratives. In Matthew 9:22, Jesus tells a woman who was healed of a hemorrhage, ". . . your faith has made you well." (See also Mark 5:34 and Luke 8:48).

Her faith was the cause of healing transmission. What did her faith look like? In verse twenty-one, there is a description of her faith. Her faith was, "If I only touch His garment, I will get well." There is no description that her faith was in the deity of Jesus, although it may be assumed. She initiated her faith. Her faith was for a specific request. She wanted to be healed. One might assume that she believed in the deity of Jesus. She had heard of Jesus, although the Scripture does not reveal what she knew of Jesus. Whatever she had been told about Jesus ignited faith in her to touch Jesus' garment so she could be healed.

A second narrative that demonstrates faith's role in healing is found in Acts 14. Here a lame man is listening to Paul preach. Acts 14:9 says that Paul saw "that he had faith to be made well." Paul commanded him to stand, and he was healed. This brings up two issues that pertain to this project. The first issue is that according to verse nine, the ". . . man was listening to Paul as he spoke . . ." Was this pointed out to indicate a possible connection to faith being kindled in the man as he heard Paul preach? It might be assumed that Paul was preaching about Jesus as he did in verse three. Is it too much to assume that as Paul was preaching, faith came alive for him to be healed? Secondly, the lame man's faith was for a specific request. He wanted to be healed. His faith, though assumed to be directed to Jesus, was not just in His deity but for a specific request: healing.

The role of faith in these two narratives has a couple of similarities. First, the afflicted person's faith was for healing. Secondly, their faith, not Jesus' or Paul's, resulted in their healing.

Faith Not Present in Healing Narrative

The New Testament records a story in which faith is not mentioned concerning a miracle. In Luke 7, there is a story of a widow mourning her only son, who is dead. In verse 13, Luke reveals that Jesus felt compassion for her. Jesus then takes the initiative. He speaks words of comfort to her. He touches the coffin. He speaks to her son and commands him to arise. One might first observe that this story does not mention faith. Secondly, it is observed that Jesus was not asked or approached in any way. It was simply His compassionate response for her to release His power to bring life back to the dead man.

This project does not intend to make a distinction between healing and miracles. It is not known why the man died. Was Jesus healing a disease that killed him, or was He helping him to supernaturally recover from an accident? Whether one concludes this is a healing or a miracle, the story illustrates the sovereign will of God and the divine love of God that initiated and completed this miracle.

Unbelief Responsible for Limitation of the Miraculous

When Jesus returned to His hometown, the Bible records a controversial situation. In Matthew 13:58 it says that Jesus ". . . did not do many miracles . . ." Mark 6:5 says that Jesus ". . . could do no miracle . . ." although He did heal a few people. What was the cause of the limitation of the miraculous in Jesus' hometown? Mark remarks that Jesus observed unbelief. Matthew is more explicit when he says it was ". . . because of their unbelief." Unbelief was the cause or was present in the situation where Jesus' miracle power was limited. Unbelief can be a reason for the limitation of miraculous power.

The Mystery of Faith

How can one know the role of faith as it relates to the subject of divine healing? Many times, maybe most times, in Scripture, faith played a role. There seem to be occasions in Scripture where faith is not present or mentioned regarding the person receiving healing. The exact role that faith plays in divine healing is a mystery. It is because of this mystery that one must consider two significant thoughts. Number one, it should never be assumed that when healing does not occur, it is an issue of faith on the part of the one seeking healing. Number two, one should never feel condemned concerning faith as the only issue about the transmission and the receiving of healing. I want to emphasize God and His desire to care for the needs of humanity while simultaneously acknowledging the role of faith in the healing available through the atonement.

Faith Comes by Preaching

Why is teach, preach, and heal model useful? The literature would suggest that one of the many reasons this model was effective for Jesus and will be effective for the church today is that it develops faith. Wesley Baldwin suggests that this reason was why the historical church survived. The teaching and preaching of its leadership continually stoked faith.[80] Ward echoes this effect when someone is dealing with internal wounds. Hearing the preached word brings comfort and psychologically prepares one for healing.[81] When commenting on why preaching is so paramount,

---

80   Wesley Baldwin, "The Centrality of Preaching in Christian Worship" (PhD diss., Southwestern Baptist Theological Seminary, Fort Worth, TX, 2015), 82, ProQuest Dissertations & Theses Global.

81   Ward, "Our Lives as Well," 6.

he says, "Faith on the part of the one in crisis is paramount to receiving healing."[82] Jesus taught to develop faith in the hearers. That faith helped people receive healing from Him.

Faith and Healing

It is a fact that faith facilitates receiving divine healing. Jones writes in his article, "If we repeatedly search the healings of Jesus, we note that He rewards people's faith as a vital role in their healing."[83] Though this is often misunderstood and used as an insult for lack of manifestation, it is a prominent factor. Healings in the pericopes were affected by the faith of those who received healing.

While there seems to be a minimal number of exceptions, as a rule, it is hard to miss the role of faith for healing. David Ward notes that preaching was "one practice among many Christian practices that constitute an interconnected whole, a way of life, and a way of knowing."[84] He brings out that preaching stimulated faith for "educational, therapeutic, and soteriological"[85] purposes.

His primary focus is the healing of the inner person. This does not divert us from understanding the healing of the whole person is part and parcel to the divine healing experience that God desires for His people. One can draw from his writings that the preaching/teaching that facilitates the healing of the inner person will also promote the healing of the outer person. One can receive healing by faith in the present. There is faith for future blessings as well.

82   Jones, "The Healing Power," 44.

83   Jones, "The Healing Power," 40.

84   David Ward, "Our Lives as Well: Teaching Preaching as a Formative Christian Practice," (PhD diss., Princeton Theological Seminary, Princeton, New Jersey, 2012), Abstract, ProQuest Dissertations & Theses Global.

85   Ward, "Our Lives as Well," 12.

The Power of Faith in Wholeness

Faith is not a passive belief; it is a dynamic force that transforms lives. The story in Acts 14:7-10 gives us a profound illustration of faith's ability to bring about wholeness. A man, lame from birth, experienced a miraculous healing—not through medicine or human intervention, but through faith ignited by the preaching of the gospel.

This chapter explores the nature of faith, its power to restore, and how we can cultivate faith that leads to wholeness in our own lives.

Faith Begins with Recognizing Our Need

Before faith can bring wholeness, we must first recognize our condition. The lame man in Lystra was not just physically disabled—he was bound by limitations that defined his entire existence. The Scripture emphasizes his condition in multiple ways: he had no strength in his feet, he was lame from birth, and he had never walked (Acts 14:8). This repetition is significant because it underscores the totality of his need.

Many of us live with unseen limitations—emotional wounds, spiritual struggles, or ingrained habits that hinder our full potential. Sometimes, we become so accustomed to our struggles that we fail to recognize our need for change. Yet, faith begins with an honest acknowledgment: we need something greater than ourselves.

As Jesus said, "Blessed are the poor in spirit, for theirs is the kingdom of heaven" (Matthew 5:3). Until we recognize our need, we will not seek transformation.

The Condition of the Lame Man

Acts 14:8 describes the man's state in three distinct ways:

"He had no strength in his feet" – He lacked the ability to stand or move on his own.

"Lame from his mother's womb" – His condition was lifelong; it was not temporary or due to an accident.

"Had never walked" – He had never experienced the ability to stand, move, or live like others.

The repetition in this verse is not accidental. It emphasizes the depth of his need. He was completely dependent on others, unable to change his circumstances, and had no prior experience of mobility. He was not just weak—he was entirely unable.

Many of us, though not physically lame, are in a similar spiritual, emotional, or even mental state. We have areas in our lives where we are stuck, unable to move forward, or limited by past experiences, fear, or wounds. Yet, we often fail to acknowledge these limitations. We accept our condition as normal, just as the lame man had likely adjusted to his immobility as an unavoidable reality.

Recognizing Our Need is the First Step Toward Faith

The first step to wholeness is acknowledging where we truly are. Jesus said in Matthew 9:12, "It is not the healthy who need a doctor, but the sick."

Many times, we resist recognizing our spiritual, emotional, or personal struggles because:

We have become comfortable in our dysfunction.

We compare ourselves with others and think, "I'm not as bad as them".

We have been in the same situation for so long that we lose hope of change.

We fear admitting our struggles because it makes us feel weak or inadequate.

However, Scripture teaches that the moment we acknowledge our weakness, God's strength is made available. Paul writes in 2 Corinthians 12:9, "My grace is sufficient for you, for my power is made perfect in weakness." It is not until we come to terms with our need for healing, deliverance, and transformation that we can step into the faith that brings wholeness.

The Danger of Spiritual Blindness

One of the greatest obstacles to faith is not recognizing our need. In Revelation 3:17, Jesus rebukes the Laodicean church, saying: "You say, 'I am rich; I have acquired wealth and do not need a thing.' But you do not realize that you are wretched, pitiful, poor, blind and naked."

This passage reveals a critical truth: we can be spiritually needy but unaware of it. This kind of spiritual blindness is dangerous because it prevents us from seeking the faith that leads to transformation.

The Pharisees in Jesus' time also fell into this trap. They believed they were spiritually strong because of their religious status, but Jesus said to them in John 9:41, "If you were blind, you would not be guilty of sin; but now that you claim you can see, your guilt remains."

It is better to admit our weakness and seek God's help than to pretend we are fine and miss His power. The lame man in Acts 14 knew he was crippled, and that awareness prepared him to receive a miracle.

How We Can Recognize Our Need

Just as the lame man had to acknowledge his condition before receiving healing, we must examine our own lives. Here are some questions to reflect on:

Are there areas in my life where I feel stuck, powerless, or broken?

Am I avoiding dealing with certain struggles because they seem too difficult to change?

Have I accepted dysfunction as my reality instead of believing for something better?

Am I humble enough to acknowledge that I need God's help?

The good news is that God never exposes our need to condemn us—He does it to heal us. Just as the lame man in Acts 14 was not left in his condition, God does not leave us in ours.

The moment we recognize our need, we are positioned to experience the power of faith that brings transformation.

Faith Comes Through Hearing the Word

The miracle in Acts 14 did not begin with the man's effort—it began with preaching. Paul preached the gospel in Lystra, and as he spoke, the lame man listened intently. The turning point was when Paul perceived that he had faith to be made well (Acts 14:9). This tells us something critical: faith is not self-generated; it is ignited through the Word of God.

Romans 10:17 confirms this: "So faith comes from hearing, and hearing by the word of Christ." The gospel is more than a message of salvation—it is a message of restoration, healing, and divine possibility. When we engage with the Word of God—whether through preaching, reading, or personal devotion—our faith is strengthened.

The Nature of Faith

Faith is not just belief in God's existence; it is belief for something. Hebrews 11:6 tells us: "Without faith, it is impossible to please [God], for he who comes to God must believe that He is and that He is a rewarder of those who seek Him." Faith is twofold:

Belief in God's reality

Belief in God's response

The lame man's faith was not vague—it was faith to be made well. He believed that God could and would heal him. Faith must always have an object; it must be directed toward God's promises.

Faith is not something we manufacture on our own—it is ignited by hearing the Word of God. The story of the lame man in Acts 14:7-10 illustrates this principle powerfully. This man had been crippled from birth, never knowing what it was like to walk. Yet, something extraordinary happened when he heard the gospel preached by Paul.

The Bible tells us that while Paul was speaking, he "fixed his gaze on him and saw that he had faith to be made well" (Acts 14:9). Where did this faith come from? It was not something the man had been born with—it came through hearing the Word of God. This chapter explores how faith is born, how it grows, and how it leads to transformation.

Faith is Born Through the Word

Romans 10:17 clearly states: "So faith comes from hearing, and hearing by the word of Christ."

Faith does not originate from feelings, emotions, or personal willpower. Instead, it is a response to God's Word. When the gospel is preached, it reveals truth, exposes the character of God, and awakens faith in the hearts of those who hear.

The lame man in Acts 14 was listening as Paul spoke. He didn't just passively hear the words—he absorbed them, believed them, and faith was ignited in his heart. This shows us a key principle: when we position ourselves to hear the Word of God, faith begins to grow.

The Power of Preaching

The Bible repeatedly emphasizes that God uses preaching to stir faith in people's hearts.

Acts 14:7 – "And there they continued to preach the gospel."

Acts 14:21 – "After they had preached the gospel to that city and had made many disciples…"

Preaching is not just a religious practice—it is God's chosen method of communicating life-changing truth. 1 Corinthians 1:21 says, "God was pleased through the foolishness of what was preached to save those who believe."

It is through preaching and teaching of the Word that people come to faith. The lame man in Lystra experienced a miracle because he heard the message of Christ and believed.

Hearing the Word is More Than Just Listening

It's important to recognize that not everyone who hears the Word experiences faith. Jesus often said, "He who has ears to hear, let him hear!" (Matthew 11:15).

This means that hearing is not just about physically listening—it is about receiving, understanding, and believing. James 1:22 warns us: "Do not merely listen to the word, and so deceive yourselves. Do what it says."

Many people hear sermons, read Scripture, or listen to teachings but remain unchanged because they do not actively engage with what they hear. The lame man in Acts 14 had ears to hear—he listened with an open heart, and faith was birthed in him.

Faith is Strengthened Through Repeated Exposure to the Word

Faith does not just appear once and remain strong forever. Like a muscle, faith must be exercised and strengthened. This happens through continuous hearing and meditating on the Word of God.

Daily Intake of God's Word Builds Faith

Just as food nourishes the body, the Word of God nourishes our faith. Deuteronomy 8:3 says, "Man shall not live by bread alone, but by every word that proceeds out of the mouth of God." If we neglect the Word, our faith becomes weak. But when we consistently hear, read, and meditate on Scripture, our faith grows stronger.

The Example of Abraham: Growing in Faith

Romans 4:20-21 describes how Abraham's faith grew over time: "Yet he did not waver through unbelief regarding the promise of God, but was strengthened in his faith and gave glory to God, being fully persuaded that God had power to do what He had promised."

How did Abraham's faith grow? He continued to believe God's promises. The more we hear and meditate on God's Word, the more our faith deepens and strengthens.

Faith Must Be Rooted in the Right Source

Not all hearing produces faith. In today's world, we hear many voices—news, social media, opinions, fears, doubts. If we listen more to the voices of the world than to the Word of God, our faith will weaken.

The question is: What are we feeding our faith?

Are we filling our minds with God's promises or with fear and doubt?

Are we listening to the Word of truth or the voices of negativity?

Philippians 4:8 instructs us: "Whatever is true, whatever is noble, whatever is right, whatever is pure, whatever is lovely, whatever is admirable—if anything is excellent or praiseworthy—think about such things."

If we want to grow in faith, we must intentionally listen to and meditate on God's Word, rather than being consumed by the distractions of the world.

Faith in Action: Responding to the Word

Hearing the Word without action is ineffective. True faith responds.

The lame man in Acts 14 heard, believed, and acted.

Peter, when Jesus called him to walk on water, heard, believed, and stepped out (Matthew 14:28-29).

The woman with the issue of blood in Mark 5 heard about Jesus, believed, and pressed through the crowd to touch Him.

Faith without action is incomplete. James 2:26 says, "Faith without works is dead."

When we hear the Word, we must respond in obedience, whether it's stepping out in faith, trusting God's promises, or making decisions based on His truth.

The story of the lame man in Acts 14 teaches us that faith is not self-generated—it is born through hearing the Word of God.

Faith is ignited when we listen to God's Word with an open heart.

Faith grows stronger through continual exposure to Scripture.

Faith is weakened when we fill our minds with the voices of doubt.

Faith must be acted upon to be effective.

If we desire to grow in faith, we must immerse ourselves in the Word daily. The more we hear, believe, and respond, the stronger our faith will become. Just as the lame man in Acts 14 listened, believed, and was healed, we too can experience the power of faith by hearing and acting upon the Word of God.

Faith Requires Action

Faith is never passive. When Paul saw the man's faith, he did not merely encourage him to believe harder—he called him to action: "Stand upright on your feet!" (Acts 14:10) At that moment, the man had a choice: to stay seated in his familiar condition or to act on his faith.

Faith always demands a response.

James 2:26 reinforces this truth: "For just as the body without the spirit is dead, so also faith without works is dead." Faith is not complete until it is put into action. Whether it is stepping out in obedience, praying with expectation, or making bold decisions based on God's Word, our faith is proven through our actions.

Faith in Trials: Enduring to the Promise

Faith is not just about one moment of obedience; it requires perseverance. Acts 14:21-23 shows how Paul and Barnabas encouraged the disciples to continue in the faith, even through tribulations. Faith is not just for miracles—it is for the long journey of life.

2 Timothy 3:12 reminds us: "Indeed, all who desire to live godly in Christ Jesus will be persecuted." Faith does not exempt us from challenges; it empowers us to overcome them. True faith is enduring faith—faith that holds firm even when circumstances seem contrary to God's promises.

Faith is not merely a belief—it is a force that requires action. In the story of the lame man in Acts 14:7-10, we see a powerful demonstration of this truth. The man had faith to be healed, but his healing did not manifest until he acted upon that faith. When Paul perceived his faith, he didn't just acknowledge it—he commanded the man to take action: "Stand upright on your feet!" (Acts 14:10)

At that moment, the man had a choice: he could stay seated, doubting whether he could stand, or he could trust the word spoken over him and act. The moment he acted—he leaped up and walked—his faith was fulfilled.

This story teaches us a critical lesson: faith without action is incomplete. It is not enough to believe in God's promises; we must step out in obedience, trusting Him to bring His Word to fulfillment.

Faith is Proved by Action

Many people think of faith as an internal conviction, but Scripture consistently teaches that true faith is always accompanied by action. James 2:17 declares: "Faith by itself, if it does not have works, is dead." Faith is not just believing in God—it is acting upon His Word. Consider these biblical examples:

Noah had faith that God would bring a flood, but his faith was demonstrated when he built the ark (Hebrews 11:7).

Abraham had faith in God's promise, but that faith was completed when he left his homeland and later offered Isaac (Hebrews 11:8, 17).

Peter had faith that Jesus could sustain him on the water, but he had to step out of the boat before the miracle happened (Matthew 14:28-29).

In each case, faith was not passive—it was active. They did not just believe; they took steps of obedience.

Faith Requires Risk

Acting on faith often requires stepping into the unknown. The lame man in Acts 14 had never walked before. His entire life had been spent in immobility. When Paul commanded him to stand, he had no prior experience of walking to rely on—all he had was the Word spoken to him.

This is the nature of faith—it requires trusting in what we do not yet see. Hebrews 11:1 defines faith as: "The assurance of things hoped for, the conviction of things not seen."

Many times, God will call us to take a step before we see any evidence of His promise. This can feel risky, but it is the very essence of faith.

Moses had to stretch out his staff before the Red Sea parted (Exodus 14:16).

The priests carrying the Ark had to step into the Jordan River before the waters stopped flowing (Joshua 3:13).

The widow at Zarephath had to use her last bit of flour and oil before God provided abundantly (1 Kings 17:13-14).

In each case, action preceded the miracle. The same is true for us—our faith is activated when we take action on God's Word.

Faith and Obedience Go Hand in Hand

Faith is not about testing God—it is about obeying Him. Some people wait for every detail to be clear before they act in faith, but God often asks us to step out before we see the full picture.

Abraham is called the father of faith because he obeyed before having all the answers. Hebrews 11:8 says: "By faith Abraham obeyed when he was called to go out to a place that he was to receive as an inheritance. And he went out, not knowing where he was going."

Faith does not demand full understanding—it requires trust in God's leading. If we only obey when everything makes sense, we are not walking by faith, but by sight (2 Corinthians 5:7).

Faith in Action Brings Wholeness

In Acts 14, the lame man received wholeness the moment he acted on his faith. This principle is consistent throughout Scripture:

The ten lepers were healed as they went to show themselves to the priest (Luke 17:14).

The blind man was healed after he obeyed Jesus and washed in the pool of Siloam (John 9:7).

The woman with the issue of blood received healing when she pressed through the crowd and touched Jesus' garment (Mark 5:27-29).

God's power is available, but it is activated through our obedience.

Faith Requires Perseverance

Taking the first step of faith is important, but true faith requires endurance. Paul and Barnabas encouraged the new believers in Acts 14:22, saying: "Through many tribulations we must enter the kingdom of God." Faith is not just about believing once; it is about continuing to believe, even when challenges arise.

- Joseph held onto his faith for years before seeing his dream fulfilled.
- David was anointed king long before he actually took the throne.
- The early church faced persecution, but they continued to walk in faith.

True faith does not waver when trials come—it presses on, trusting that God will fulfill His promises.

Practical Ways to Put Faith into Action

Faith is not just an abstract concept—it is something we live out daily. Here are some ways we can put faith into action:

1. Obey God's Word

When Scripture commands something, we should act on it immediately. Whether it is forgiving someone, tithing, sharing the gospel, or trusting God in difficulty, faith is proven through obedience.

2. Take Bold Steps

God may be calling you to start a ministry, switch careers, step into leadership, or trust Him in a new way. Do not wait for everything to be perfect—take the first step in faith.

3. Pray with Expectation

Pray as though God is listening and will answer. Faith-filled prayers are not empty words; they are spoken with confidence in God's promises (Mark 11:24).

4. Speak and Declare God's Promises

Faith is released through our words. Speak life, healing, provision, and strength over your situation. Proverbs 18:21 says: "The power of life and death is in the tongue."

5. Refuse to Give Up

Doubt will try to creep in, but hold onto faith. Stand on God's Word, not your circumstances.

The story in Acts 14 is more than a historical event; it is a model for our own lives. Faith is the key to wholeness—spiritually, emotionally, and even physically.

Recognize your need – Do not settle for less than God's best.

Immerse yourself in the Word – Faith is built by hearing and believing the Word of God.

Act on your faith – Faith without action is incomplete.

Persevere through challenges – True faith is enduring faith.

The same God who healed the lame man in Lystra is still at work today. Faith makes the impossible possible. Will you believe? Will you step out in faith? The choice is yours.

CHAPTER 5

Biblical Foundations for TPH Model

This book maintains that if believers seeking divine healing commit to daily reading and/or listening to sermons about divine healing, their healing experience will be enhanced. The following pages present a pneumatological reflection from a Biblical perspective concerning this project. This project discusses the Old Testament and the New Testament approach to healing. Then four pericopes are examined. The first is a mirrored pair of pericopes found in Matthew 4:23–25 and Matthew 9:35,38. These are the basis of developing a model of receiving divine healing. The second pericope is Isaiah 53:4–5. This famous passage establishes that healing is in the atonement of Jesus Christ. The third pericope is Romans 10:16–17. Paul writes that through hearing the Word of God, one receives faith, which is usually necessary to receive divine healing. The fourth pericope is Proverbs 4:20–22. This Old Testament witness further supports the significance of hearing the Word of God and its connection to receiving healing in the body. This book then summarizes how these pericopes apply to the project.

Old Testament Overview of Healing

God revealed Himself as a healing God in the Old Testament, and healing manifested in various ways. In Exodus 15:26, God said, ". . . I, the LORD, am your healer." Karl Barth called this the Magna Carta of healing in the OT.[86] This project examines the OT healing theology in several diverse ways. The first is the numerous characteristics of health in the OT. Next, the OT uses three major words for healing and health. Third, there are several different ways divine healing is transmitted. Fourth, five noteworthy observations about Exodus 15:26 inform this project. Finally, the OT gives an essential description of all sicknesses in Deuteronomy 28.

OT Characteristics of Healing and Health

The three characteristics of healing and health in OT are significant for this project. The first is peace, as translated from the Hebrew word shalom (שׁולם). Included in its meaning is the idea of well-being.[87] The Bible mentions shalom (שׁולם) over 250 times. It can also mean prosperity, health, and completeness. Its range of meaning includes spiritual, mental, physical, and economic areas.[88] The second characteristic of health and healing in the OT is strength. It occurs over 130 times.[89] It includes human energy and vitality. Psalm 29:11 calls strength a gift from God. Adamo says that God's strength is nuanced to mean total wellness.[90] The third characteristic of health and healing in the OT is fertility. In Deuteronomy 7:12–14, God promises fertility to those who

---

86   David T. Adamo, "'I Am the LORD Your Healer' Exodus 15:26 (ראפרהוהיינא): Healing in the Old Testament and the African (Yoruba) Context," *In Die Skriflig* 55, no. 1 (May 1, 2021): 3, https://doi:10.4102/ids.v55i1.2689.

87   Adamo, "I Am the LORD," 2.

88   Adamo, "I Am the LORD," 2.

89   Adamo, "I Am the LORD," 3.

90   Adamo, "I Am the LORD," 3.

obey the commandments of God. In essence, those who love God would never be barren. Finally, the OT will speak of the longevity of life to those who adhere to God. Longevity is a result of good health. According to Psalm 91:16, those who worship and love, and show faith in God receive the promise of long life.

Three Major Words for Healing in the OT

According to Adamo, three significant words in the OT refer to God restoring health to a person. The most used word is healing.[91] Exodus 15:26 points to God as the One Who causes health and recovery of health. Its root means "to stitch together," as in putting flesh back together.[92] The following two words are significant but not used often. The word translated cure. It is used over 15 times in the OT. It refers to the restoration of the soundness of health. Divine healing eliminates the symptoms and removes the root problem. The final word, binding, as in Hosea 6:1, means to cover a wound with a bandage that will promote progressive healing and prevent further physical problems.[93]

OT Ways Healing is Transmitted

The OT reveals several different ways people experienced healing. First, words transmit healing.[94] God spoke to Abraham that he would have a son. (Gen. 18:10) God healed Abimelech in response to the prayer of Abraham. (Gen. 20:17) A son was born to a barren Shunammite woman by way of Elisha's declaration. (2 Kings 4:8–17) The second method of healing transmitted in the OT was by touch or body contact. Elijah healed a widow's son by lying on him. (1 Kings 7:20–21) Elisha's

---

91   Adamo, "I Am the LORD," 3.
92   Adamo, "I Am the LORD," 3.
93   Adamo, "I Am the LORD," 3.
94   Adamo, "I Am the LORD," 4.

protégé followed suit when he raised a boy from the dead by putting his mouth on his mouth, eyes on his eyes, and hands on his hands. (2 Kings 4:18–36) Material means is the third way people received healing in the OT.

In Exodus 15:26, undrinkable water is made drinkable by inserting a tree limb. In Isaiah 38:21, Hezekiah was to "take a cake of figs" and apply it to a boil for healing. Fourth, when a person looks at a bronze serpent, they receive healing. (Num. 21:4–9) The released snakes punished people for murmuring against God. God's remedy when a person got bitten by a snake was to look at a bronze serpent in the middle of the encampment. Adamo states that the snakes were messengers of God to punish.[95] God, in His mercy, intervened by looking at the bronze serpent on a pole. This is undoubtedly a picture of foreshadowing Jesus being on the cross.

Five Observations About Exodus 15:26

This project makes five observations about Exodus 15:26. The first is that healing is a condition of obedience. The second observation is that God wanted to prevent diseases from coming on to His obedient people. The diseases the people of God would encounter would be the same as those that came upon the Egyptian people. Fourth, God, Himself appears to inflict diseases. Finally, there is an assurance that God can and wants to heal His people when they get sick.

The OT View of Sickness as a Curse

In the OT, people describe sickness as a curse. Deuteronomy 28:61 says, "Also every sickness and every plague which, not written in the

---

95   Adamo, "I Am the LORD," 6.

book of this law, the LORD will bring on you until you are destroyed." This is in the curse section of Deuteronomy 28. The first part of this chapter describes the blessings of obedience (v. 1–14). The second part of the chapter describes the curses of disobedience (v. 15–68). The primary focus of this project is from verses in the NT. The NT addresses the Deuteronomy 28 curses. One specific scripture that addresses these curses is Galatians 3:13. It says, "Christ redeemed us from the curse of the Law, having become a curse for us for it is written, 'CURSED IS EVERYONE WHO HANGS ON A TREE.'" Deuteronomy 28:61 describes all sickness as part of the curse of the Law. Christ has redeemed Christians from the curse of the Law (Gal. 3:13). One could conclude that Christ has redeemed Christians from the curse of sickness. As addressed earlier in this book, this is to be understood as positionally available but not altogether realized. While Christians remain in the tension between the now and not yet aspect of Kingdom reality, understanding the truth of redemption of the curse demonstrates the attitude of God toward sickness and His saints.

New Testament Overview of Healing

The theology of healing in the OT root of Exodus 15:26 becomes NT fruit in James 5:14–15. The inspired writer, James, codifies several areas of the theological and practical understanding of the NT. He lays out the ongoing battle that NT believers have with sickness. However, that battle is just that, a battle. It is to be confronted. He also lays out the intentionality of the infirmed believer and the church's elders.[96] Both had a role to play in the battle for health. Then he reiterates a methodology of the transmission of healing, i.e., anointing with oil and the prayer of faith. He intertwines the prayer of faith for healing and the forgiveness of sin. These points lay out an overview of healing in the NT.

---

96   Ervin, *Healing*, 81.

The NT Views Sickness as a Battle

Sickness is an ongoing battle for both believers and non-believers. The NT does not run away from the constant struggle with sickness. The NT does not allude that a true believer will never deal with sickness. James never shames the believer who is sick. There is no such language of rebuke to the sick person. There is no intimation of scolding, such as, "If you were living right, you would not have gotten sick." There is just a statement of acknowledgment that believers will be confronted with sickness while giving instructions on what to do within this reality. What is also missing in James' instruction is the mindset that the infirmed believer should accept sickness passively or that God placed the sickness upon them or questioned whether God might not want them healed. It is simply an instruction to confront sickness with a prayer of faith and to expect healing to occur. This simple treatment of sickness demonstrates how much the NT battles with sickness.

The New Testament View of the Minister and the Sick Person

The NT puts the onus on both the minister and the infirmed believer. In Matthew 10, Jesus commissions the twelve disciples. His instruction to them was, "Heal the sick . . ." (Matt. 10:7) However, in Matthew 17, there was an instance of them not bringing a cure to a boy when they attempted to do so. Jesus did bring a rebuke. It was not to the father of the boy or the boy. Jesus rebuked the disciples because of the "littleness of your faith . . ." (Matt. 17:20) In this narrative, the disciples were the ministers, and it was evident that their faith, or lack of faith, was involved in the healing of the boy. The statement directed toward the disciples, "your faith has made you well" (Matt. 9:22), creates a partnership between the minister and the infirmed believer. One can see this faith connection between the minister and the sick person in the ministry of Jesus in His hometown. Mark writes that Jesus "could do no miracle . . ." (Mk 6:5), and the reason given in verse six is ". . . their unbelief." Mark writes that Jesus, with His perfect faith, was unable to do any miracles because of the people's unbelief.

Faith and Healing in the NT

Faith is an essential part of NT healing. Irvin states that the prayer of faith mentioned in James closely relates to the faith pointed out in healing narratives in the Gospels.[97] This project expands the topic of faith in other parts. Some could consider James' designation of the prayer of faith as a prerequisite for healing. Although faith's exact role in a person receiving healing is debatable, the prayer of faith is part of the theology of divine healing.

Forgiveness and Healing in the NT

James makes a rather interesting connection between the prayer of faith for healing and the forgiveness of sin. Why is this connection being made by James? This book's position is that James' theology of healing was that at the same time Jesus died for the forgiveness of sin, He also paid for the healing from sickness according to the messianic prophecy in Isaiah 53. This is one of the foundations of healing in the atonement doctrine.

Judith Hill's articles provides a summary of healing in the NT.[98] She writes that NT teaches that sickness is a human reality due to the Fall. Healing is always possible by the power of God in the Name of Jesus Christ. Therefore, no sickness or injury is too difficult for God

---

97   Ervin, *Healing*, 77.

98   Judith L. Hill, "Health, Sickness and Healing in the New Testament: A Brief Theology," Africa Journal of Evangelical Theology 27, no. 1 (2008): 151.

to remedy. Healing can result through various means or a combination of scientific and supernatural means, as demonstrated in Paul's instruction to Timothy to use wine to relieve digestive issues. (1 Tim. 5:23) The techniques of receiving healing are varied depending upon the circumstances. The scripture does not always tie spiritual health to physical health. Exorcisms and healing display God's power (Matt. 15:31). According to OT prophecy, healings in the NT demonstrate that Jesus is the Messiah (Is. 53:4–5, Matt. 8:16–17). The consummation of the Kingdom of God will remove the curse's effects (Rev. 22:3). Believers must value their spiritual life, realizing it has more lasting significance than their physical life (1 Tim. 4:8).

Exegesis of Isaiah 53:4–5

The foundational pericope of the "healing in the atonement" doctrine is Isaiah 53:4–5. It reads, "Surely our griefs He Himself bore, And our sorrows He carried; Yet we ourselves esteemed Him stricken, smitten of God, and afflicted. But He was pierced through for our transgressions; He was crushed for our iniquities; The chastening for our well-being [fell] upon Him, And by His scourging, we are healed." In discussing healing in the atonement from Isaiah, Nihinlola points out that the overall view of the book of Isaiah is redemption.[99] In Isaiah, God is both Judge and Redeemer. In 53:4–5, the Suffering Servant (Jesus Christ) takes stripes and sicknesses for those who need to be redeemed. He notes that although it is clear that the Suffering Servant died for the forgiveness of sin, it is also clear that He died for the physical healing of sicknesses. Commentator Ivan Friesen emphatically states that it is clear that Jesus "took on Himself others' diseases and pain caused by their own sin."[100] This is a crucial connection: sins and sicknesses.

---

99   Nihinlola, "By His Wounds," 21.

100   Ivan Friesen, *Isaiah: Believers Church Bible Commentary* (Scottdale, Pa: Herald Press, 2009), 328.

Nihinlola also points out the connection between sin and sickness by teaching that the origin of sickness is sin.[101] Understanding the origin of sickness is monumental to the overall thrust of understanding receiving healing, as described in this book.

Humanity's rebellion against God in the Garden is the source of illnesses. Satan's successful deception of the first couple causes a separation that opens the door to all disease. Therefore, the theology of "healing is in the atonement" is the antidote. Nihinlola describes that since sickness is sourced by sin, with the removal of the source, so is its consequence, sickness. He writes, "In the healing ministry of Jesus, on the basis of redemption, we find a perfect harmony between healing and atonement."[102] Some contend that these verses only refer to the inner person's healing. To interpret whether this verse is only about the forgiveness of sin or whether it also includes the healing of a physical body, one needs to look no further than Matthew 8. In Matthew 8:14–16, Jesus heals Peter's mother-in-law. It also says that many people came to Him that night, and He "healed all that were sick." Verse 17 is poignant, "[This was] to fulfill what was spoken through Isaiah the prophet: 'HE HIMSELF TOOK OUR INFIRMITIES AND CARRIED AWAY OUR DISEASES.'" Matthew connected the physical healing of diseases to Isaiah 53:4. Nihinlola brings in an OT example, a metaphor for Jesus dying on the cross, and provides healing for people in the Gospel of John. He compares Jesus to Moses, lifting a snake on a pole.[103] As the people would look at the snake on the pole, they received healing. So, this reveals a metaphor for sin and sickness being taken care of by Jesus on the cross.

---

101   Nihinlola, "By His Wounds," 23.

102   Nihinlola, "By His Wounds," 24.

103   Nihinlola, "By His Wounds," 24.

Isaiah 53:4–5 demonstrates healing in the atonement. The same blood shed deals with the source of sickness for forgiveness. The healing mentioned in this pericope is not just internal but also external. It is foundational to the thesis as being able to be accessed in the same way forgiveness of sin is accessed.

Exegesis of Romans 10:16–17

So, how one accesses salvation is the same as how someone accesses healing. Enter the third pericope, Romans 10:16–17, "However, they did not all heed the good news; for Isaiah says, 'LORD, WHO HAS BELIEVED OUR REPORT?' So, faith [comes] from hearing, and hearing by the word of Christ." Paul Achtemeier states that one of the most significant issues of these verses is the focus on hearing.[104] He writes, "But even had the New Testament been available so that people could have read it, that would not have served as a substitute for the apostolic preaching."[105] Even though Paul wrote letters that would eventually become part of the NT, he believed that his physical presence and preaching would be far superior to the letters, see Romans 1:9–13. Achtemeier thinks that Paul is saying that hearers bear a burden to listen, and preachers are obligated to preach.[106] "One's relationship with God may depend on how carefully one listens and understands what is being said! Therefore, our passage implies a warning against careless hearing, since hearing is the key to trust in God."[107] Paul emphasized preaching's role in igniting faith in the hearer. He says that in preaching and hearing God's Word, one can respond to God appropriately.[108] This pericope

---

104   Paul J. Achtemeier, *Romans*, Interpretation, a Bible Commentary for Teaching and Preaching (Atlanta: Westminster John Knox Press, 1985), 173.

105   Achtemeier, *Romans*, 173.

106   Achtemeier, *Romans*, 174.

107   Achtemeier, *Romans*, 175.

108   Achtemeier, *Romans*, 176.

supports the thesis of this project of the importance of hearing preaching to help one have faith. Preaching and hearing about Jesus and His atoning work is an essential connection in transmitting divine healing.

Textual criticism of this verse is necessary. There are a couple of variations in translation. Some variants translate it as "word of God" or "word of Christ." Richard Longenecker's believes the evidence supports that the "word of Christ" is original, replaced by a more acceptable "word of God."[109] He also notes the connection of this verse to Isaiah 53. He believes that Paul's inclusion of Isaiah establishes the relationship between faith and preaching.[110] The chapter establishing healing in the atonement (Is. 53) connects with the pericope establishing preaching's role in developing faith (Rom. 10:16–17).

The thesis states that Christ's activity of teaching, preaching, and healing is more than a description of His ministry. His earthly ministry also serves as a model for the transmission and receiving of divine healing. Is this connection between hearing the Word of God and receiving divine healing found in Scripture didactically?

Exegesis of Proverbs 4:20–22

To answer that question, this book turns to Proverbs 4:20–22. It says, "My son, give attention to my words; Incline your ear to my sayings. Do not let them depart from your sight; Keep them in the midst of your heart. For they are life to those who find them and health to all their body." Knut Heim points out that even though there are attempts to smooth over "my words" to read "understanding," it is an error. He believes the text is more focused on "turning one's ear to actual

---

109   Richard Longenecker, *The Epistle to the Romans: a Commentary on the Greek Text* (Grand Rapids: William B. Eerdmans Publishing Company, 2016), 792.

110   Longenecker, *The Epistle to the Romans*, 855.

sounds, such as those produced by spoken words."[111] Obviously, this is a critical observation given the focus of this proposal. The LXX uses the Greek word ἴασις, which translated "health."[112] The BDAG further explains that this word's range is "restoration to health after a physical malady, deliverance from a variety of ills or conditions that lie beyond physical maladies, cure, deliverance."[113] Therefore, this passage says that intentionally hearing God's Word is medicine to the physical body. Jeff Levin and Keith Meador point out that using the Torah for physical healing was practiced by the Jews.[114] They write about Rabbi Joshua ben Levi, credited with teaching about the Torah's healing power. He said,

> If he feels pains in his head, let him engage in the study of the Torah, since it is said: 'For they shall be a chaplet of grace unto your head...' If he feels pains in his throat, let him engage in the study of the Torah, since it is said: '... and chains about your neck.' If he feels pains in his bowels, let him engage in the study of the Torah, since it is said: 'It shall be a healing to your navel...' (Proverbs 3:8). If he feels pain in his bones, let him engage in the study of the Torah, since it is said: '... and marrow to your bones...'. If he feels pain in all his body, let him engage in the study of the Torah, since it is said: '... and healing to all his flesh'[115]

Levin and Meador propose that more research between the Torah and healing is needed. They said that this tradition of prescribing readings of the Torah and receiving healing is an established practice among

111   Knut Martin Heim, Poetic Imagination in Proverbs: Variant Repetitions and the Nature of Poetry (Pennsylvania State University Press, 2012), 83, ProQuest Ebook Central.

112   "G2392 - iasis - Strong's Greek Lexicon (NASB)." Blue Letter Bible, last modified September 20, 2020, https://www.blueletterbible.org//lang/lexicon/lexicon.cfm?Strongs=G2392&t=NASB.

113   Bauer and Danker, "ἴασις," in A Greek-English Lexicon of the New Testament and Other Early Christian Literature, 465.

114   Jeff Levin, and Keith Meador, Healing to All Their Flesh: Jewish and Christian Perspectives on Spirituality, Theology, and Health (West Conshohocken, Pa: Templeton Press, 2012), 107.

115   Levin, Healing to All Their Flesh, 107.

the Jewish people. This proposal might be the research they propose to be undertaken.

How These Pericopes Apply to the Proposed Model

The analysis of Biblical pericopes begs the question, "How do these passages apply to the project?" The first pericope, Matthew 4:23–25 and 9:35–38, has several functions. They set forth the description of the activity of Jesus' healing ministry. They show His dominion over sickness and disease. The repetition of the words "teach," "preach," and "healing" (in that order) put much weight on the practice. It is intentional. These verses reveal that the healed people were not just people who came once to receive healing but were followers of Jesus. They had heard Him teach many times. These verses seem to make the connection that this was intentional on Jesus' part and serve as a model for this project.

The second pericope, Isaiah 53:4–5, reveals divine healing is in the atonement. This is especially important for this project. It combats the idea that divine healing is merely up to divine whims or only dispersed through the gifts of healing. Understanding that healing is in the atonement removes the subjectivity from transmitting and receiving divine healing. Understanding that healing is in the atonement puts urgency or weight on divine healing. One might overlook its importance, knowing that all physical healing is temporary. The scrouging of Jesus demonstrates that although healing is temporary, the sick must seek Him for healing.

The third pericope, Romans 10:16–17, demonstrates the role of hearing God's Word and the development of faith. The one seeking healing almost always needs faith for healing. The thesis of this proposal summarizes that hearing preaching increases one's ability to receive healing. This verse provides the mechanism. Since faith can facilitate healing and hearing preaching produces faith, hearing preaching helps facilitate healing.

Finally, the fourth pericope, Proverbs 4:20–22, gives further support prescriptively. This verse shows that by hearing the Word of God, it can become medicine to the flesh. It also provides an example that parallels the use of the Torah and the thesis of this proposal. This verse also provides a supporting strategy to receiving healing by using meditation (. . . keep them in the midst of your heart). Meditation includes thinking about the Word of God and confessing the Word of God.[116]

Divine healing has been part of the Charismatic church since the book of Acts until now. There are many questions concerning healing. Why do some receive healing, and why do others not? This proposal does not propose to answer every question of divine healing, nor does it assume to remove the mystery of God. It does suggest examining the life and ministry of Christ as a possible model to enhance the transmission of the healing that those stripes on His back made available to humanity.

Justification for Teaching Bringing Healing as a Model

Is this just a historical record of His activities, or is this a model that the church can use today? Robert Collins maintains that not only is this an approach to healing, it is the approach to healing.[117] He tracked the use of preaching and its effects on a congregation from an emotional healing point of view. He found that preaching, particularly storytelling preaching, was the most effective tool to facilitate healing. Again, his

---

116   "What Does the Bible Say about Meditation?," Bible Study Tools, accessed November 29, 2019, https://www.biblestudytools.com/bible-study/topical-studies/what-does-the-bible-say-about-meditation.html.

117   Robert Collins, "Healing through Story: Exploring the use of Storytelling Preaching as a Means for Healing a Congregation." (PhD diss., Mercer University, Macon, GA, 2018), 17, ProQuest Dissertations & Theses Global.

observations are mainly internal and emotional, but these can be linked to whole-person healing as well. Richard Hart's article quotes Pope Francis saying, "We are to preach healing to the wounded. Be a source of healing empowerment, encouragement, and liberation."[118] Though the quote does not explicitly mention physical healing, the article identifies humanity's total healing, including physical healing.

Richard Cox explores what happens in the brain when it receives preaching and teaching.[119] The effects on a person's mind and ability to believe the things presented are very telling and applicable to receiving healing. He writes that the brain responds to repetition.[120] This is why God would say that His people would learn through a repetitive process in Isaiah 28:9–10. Cox writes concerning the importance of the sermon in helping people receive healing by saying, "The brain produces the neural connections that support or discourage the neuro connections, neurotransmitters, and neural energy for the body to either stay sick or get well. Preaching can play a vital part in allowing and helping the mind as a positive reinforcing agent for health."[121] He continues to make the point by writing,

To preach successfully regarding healing the body, a bit of knowledge about how the body responds to the spoken word is essential. Words are translated into thoughts, and thoughts become brain waves that activate neurophysiological and neurochemical channels. Hormones respond to thoughts and feelings. There is compelling evidence that how we think determines what

---

118   Richard Hart, "Preaching and Healing: Best Form of Healing is to Preach with a Spirit of Joy," *The Priest* 72, no. 8 (August 2016): 20.

119   Richard Cox, *Rewiring Your Preaching* (Downers Grove: Intervarsity Press, 2012), Preface, Kindle.

120   Cox, *Rewiring*, chap. 2.

121   Cox, *Rewiring*, chap. 13.

chemicals are activated. The proverb "For as he thinks in his heart, so is he" (Prov 23:7 Amplified Bible) is not idle information but a solemn warning. Preaching helps us to think. It has the power to set the stage for healthy thinking. It has the authority of the Scriptures and the church behind it to back up the admonition for godly treatment of the human body. Now as never before, preaching even has the power of neuroscience behind it.[122]

In summary, Cox argues that understanding the importance of consistent and convincing preaching of the Gospel, as this project proposes, will help a person seeking healing have the confidence and comfort to enhance their healing experience. Hart concurs and adds that the reason this is a duplicatable model is that there is a "comfort from the Word that brings healing."[123]

John Poirier writes an opposing view of using the healing narratives as a model for today's ministry.[124] He warns against spiritualizing the narratives on the one hand and using them as a model on the other side. He does believe in divine healing. However, he teaches that the church will make mistakes if it does not take the activities of Jesus at face value. In summary, Poirier warns that some see the healing narratives as speaking to a spiritualized truth and miss the contextual truth that a physical healing occurred. He uses the healing narrative of Bartimaeus as an example. In making his miracle a gospel in a capsule, humanity was born blind, but that salvation through Jesus makes them see, one could miss the fact that Jesus healed a man physically by allowing him to regain his sight. He maintains that truth should come from other genres of the Bible, not the narratives. He would suggest that mining truth from a narrative is problematic because there is too much room

---

122   Cox, *Rewiring*, chap. 13.

123   Hart, "Preaching," 20.

124   John Poirier, "Narrative Theology and Pentecostal Commitments," *Journal of Pentecostal Theology* 16, no. 2 (April 2008): 85. doi:10.1163/174552508X294206.

for bias. While his warning is undoubtedly something to consider, seeking practical theology from a narrative is hardly new. Nor should it be avoided altogether, especially when one can support the practical theology from other didactic portions of the Bible. Thus, this project will seek to support this model with other scriptures and assess it to verify the usefulness of this model as a model for helping people receive healing.

CHAPTER 6

Historical and Theological Reflection of Divine Healing

Divine healing is a hallmark aspect of the faith for Spirit-filled believers. However, many people do not experience divine healing on this side of heaven. Is there a way to enhance the healing experience of those seeking diving healing? To some, the recovery rate for those seeking divine healing is meager compared to the Scripture's recorded recovery rate. The purpose of the project/thesis is to equip believers to use the Christ-centered model of "teach, preach, and heal" to enhance the experience of healing to obtain a higher recovery rate for sickness resulting from divine healing. The historical and theological issues surrounding this topic by answering the following three questions. How has this issue historically been dealt with by the church? How has the church historically addressed the problem? How is the modern church addressing the issue?

Divine Healing in Church History

Divine healing has had a variety of approaches by the church through various periods in church history. Candy Brown, professor of religious studies at Indiana University, writes that throughout centuries of preaching the Gospel, divine healing has always been a declared doctrine and a practiced ministry.[125] The first period to be examined is the Ante-Nicene Church. Justin Martyr noted that many demonized and diseased people were set free by the average Christian. He said they were healed "in the name of Jesus Christ," even though the ministers did not use drugs as a treatment.[126] Tertullian mentions that the deliverance of people from demons and disease was a regular occurrence.[127] Novatian makes a point to declare that healings were "normal Christian experiences."[128] The frequency of healings and the frequency of the manifestation of the charismata in the church caused him to declare that they are "normal Christian experiences. The operation and the belief of the charismata were not an issue in his day as it was normative for the average Christian.

The second period is the Monasticism period. Monks were said to be able to produce healing.[129] Antony (251–356 AD), considered the Monastic movement's father, was said to have such a powerful prayer life that many were healed of diseases and delivered from demons.[130] Then, Ambrose (340–397 AD) observed that the gifts of healing were still operating.[131] Augustine (354–430 AD) had a ministry that included healing, raising the dead, and curing blindness, cancer, and gout.[132] In defense of the ongoing healing ministry of the church, Augustine said, "For even now miracles are wrought in the name of Christ, whether by His sacraments or by the prayers or relics of His saints; but they are not so brilliant and conspicuous as to cause them to be published with such glory as accompanied the former miracles."[133] This project examines

---

125   Candy Brown, "Jesus the Healer," *Christian History,* no. 142 (January 1, 2022): 10.

126   Eddie Hyatt, *2000 Years of Charismatic Christianity* (Lake Mary: Charisma House, 2015), 29.

127   Hyatt, *2000 Years,* 30.

128   Hyatt, *2000 Years,* 34.

129   Hyatt, *2000 Years,* 51.

130   Hyatt, *2000 Years,* 55.

131   Hyatt, *2000 Years,* 56.

132   Hyatt, *2000 Years,* 57.

133   "Church Fathers: City Of God, Book XXII (St. Augustine)," Newadvent.Org, accessed June

that healing was part of the church, even though the transmission was
not with the model.

The fourth century saw the church grow and healings diminish after
the Edict of Milan, where the church went from being persecuted to
legalized.[134] The result was a rise in nominalism and a fall in the supernatural aspect of the Gospel. Church leaders began to cast doubt on
the reality of divine healing. The body was considered a prison for
the soul, so practices of extreme asceticism became the life of deeply
committed Christians. The body was not to be cared for. They chose
sickness over healing. During that time, Jerome (347–420) translated
the Bible from Greek to Latin. James 5:15, he translated it as "save"
instead of "heal." It shifted the focus from physical healing to spiritual
healing. In the Middle Ages, church leaders restricted who could pray
for the sick or the demonized.

James 5:14–15 relegated to preparing the sick person to go to heaven.
James Bradley, professor of church history at Fuller Theological Seminary,
states that there seemed to be a decline in the volume of miraculous
healings in the late third century.[135] Some have surmised that the reduction in the miraculous was due partly to the reaction to Montanism and
the continued growth in the structure and institutional control of the
church. This is only an observation and has no objective evidence to
support the cause and effect. The negative comments of Eusebius and
Origen have caused much controversy. The negative comments seem
to indicate that the miraculous had diminished but do not state or give
any evidence. Bradley stated that the change in the legalized condition

---

15, 2018, https://www.newadvent.org/fathers/120122. htm.

134   Brown, "Jesus the Healer," 9.

135   James Bradley, "Miracles and Martyrdom in the Early Church: Some Theological and Ethical
Implications," *Pneuma* 13, no. 1 (Spr 1991): 68.

of the church correlated to the church focusing on its neediness instead of focusing on spiritual power.[136]

After a decline in the monastic movement, there was a renewal. Within the monastic revival, a Hildegard of Bingen (1098–1179), called "the most prominent woman in the Church of her day," developed an influential healing ministry.[137] She would bring healing to people who would come to her from various parts of the world. Some reported, "scarcely a sick person came to her without being healed."[138] Thomas Aquinas (1225–1274) brought some cohesiveness concerning the Catholic doctrine of divine healing.[139] He taught that healing could be obtained by the saints' intercession and through living women and holy men. He would stress that these miracles would come only by God's Power. This provided some protection against the worship of any of the people. His teaching on divine healing came with a conviction that all healings and miracles should have a religious purpose. In a sense, all healing should draw the person closer to God and His call on their life. Therefore, healing was not the real goal. The miracles should cause the healed person to respond out of gratitude toward God. They would commit to living a life of service for the Gospel. The miracle and the response of the person healed would result in the building up of the church while people would glorify Christ and surrender their lives to Him. Then there was Vincent of Ferrier (1350–1419), a powerful preacher. There were so many miracles of divine healing that they had to set aside time every day to handle the number of people who desired to be healed.[140]

---

136   Bradley, "Miracles," 72.

137   Philip Schaff, *History of the Christian Church, Volume V: The Middle Ages, A.D. 1049–1294* (Grand Rapids: William B. Eerdmans Publishing Company, 1960), 372.

138   Hyatt, *2000 Years*, 71.

139   Donald Prudlo, "Speaking with Saints," *Christian History*, no. 142 (January 1, 2022): 18.

140   Hyatt, *2000 Years*, 74.

Following the Monastic movement, Peter Waldo founded the Waldenses. In the Waldensian confession of 1431, one reads this concerning healing:

Therefore concerning the anointing of the sick, we hold it as an article of faith and profess sincerely from the heart that sick persons, when they ask it, may lawfully be anointed with anointing oil by one who joins them in praying that it may be efficacious to the healing of the body according to the design and end and effect mentioned by the apostles; and we profess that such anointing performed according to the apostolic design and practice will be healing and profitable.[141]

Next are Martin Luther (1483–1546) and the Reformation. Luther practiced praying for the sick. He would see the sick healed by calling on the name of Jesus Christ. In a famous story, God used Luther to help his friend, Philip Melanchthon, receive healing. Luther said, "Be of good courage, Philip. You shall not die."[142] He said of the healing experience of Melanchthon, "The Lord God had to stretch out his hand to me. For I threw the entire sack [of Scripture] in front of his door and rubbed his ears with all the promises to hear prayers I was able to recall from the Holy Scripture so that he had to hear me, were I to believe all those other promises."[143] A couple of years later, he announced that, through prayer, he had helped three people come back to life from the dead.[144] Luther taught ideas consistent with current faith preachers, like "faith makes us heirs" and stressing a "faith that clings to the Word of the promising God."[145] He would then pray for fellow reformer Friedrich

---

141   Hyatt, *2000 Years*, 82.

142   Hyatt, *2000 Years*, 88.

143   Ronald Rittgers, "We Have Prayed Three People to Life," *Christian History*, no. 142 (January 1, 2022): 19.

144   Rittgers, "We Have Prayed Three People to Life," 19.

145   Paul King, "A Practical-Theological Investigation of Nineteenth and Twentieth Century 'Faith Theologies'" (Doctor of Theology, University of South Africa, 2001), 21, ProQuest Dissertations & Theses Global.

Myconius and, through a letter, commanded him to recover along with the assurance that healing was God's Sovereign Will for him. However, Luther and other reformers had their doubts about divine healing. The Protestants wanted to distinguish themselves from the Catholics.[146] They removed anything that seemed to resemble Catholic superstition. Among the Protestants, there developed skepticism about divine healing. There was a particular zeal to counter any testimony about healing concerning the saints or relics. They rejected supernatural healing and the miraculous among their ranks. Luther would even argue that James 5:14–15 was from a bygone age of the church because it was rarely effective.

John Calvin (1509–1564) promoted the teaching that after the apostolic era, divine healing ceased.[147] The Gospel could spread through the Word alone. The spread of the Gospel did not need divine healing anymore. Although the Catholic Church demanded proof for their new doctrine with divine healings. Calvin said that no proof was needed. He further taught that God sent sickness. It would not make sense to combat that sickness since God sent it. Sickness should be received and even welcomed as the will of God.

According to Rittgers, this was not true of all Protestants.[148] He writes of Johann Haberman's Prayer Booklet (1565) contained sample prayers for healing. He believed that the healings at the Pool of Bethsaida (Jn 5:1–15) gave legitimacy to praying for healing. He believed that the Medieval Church had strayed from the Scriptures. He taught that as Protestants would stay faithful to the Word, they could expect divine healing.

---

146   Rittgers, "We Have Prayed Three People to Life," 20.

147   Brown, "Jesus the Healer," 9.

148   Rittgers, "We Have Prayed Three People to Life," 20.

Like Luther, others claim a healing ministry like the one proposed in this project. Madame Jeanne Guyon (1648–1717) practiced "praying the Scripture." So did George Whitefield and George Mueller.[149] Johannes Blumhardt (1805–1880) established "faith homes" to instruct those seeking healing by presenting "the Biblical message of healing within a faith-building atmosphere to enable them to obtain spiritual power over their sickness."[150] Again, very similar to the Christ-centered model for the transmission of divine healing, as presented in this project.

Divine Healing Addressed Historically in Church

This section will briefly examine how the church has addressed divine healing. This will be accomplished by first examining various models of divine healing. The models that can facilitate the MRP of "teach, preach, and heal" receive particular focus. Secondly, this book examines several factors that influenced the decline in the doctrine and practice of divine healing. Thirdly, there will be an examination of those who helped the church rediscover divine healing in the mid-1990s and one person whose teaching embodies the "teach, preach, and heal" model.

There are various models of divine healing that the church has used. A river with many streams is a description one might use to describe healing. Ronald Kydd describes six models of healing. Kydd gives examples of the various models to illustrate how they affect healing. The Confrontational Model of healing demonstrates the conflict between the dominion of darkness and the Kingdom of God. Kydd describes it as closely corresponding "to Christ's ministry."[151] The Intercessory Model of healing deals explicitly with healing transmitted by saints.[152]

---

149   King, "A Practical-Theological," 23.
150   King, "A Practical-Theological," 29.
151   Kydd, *Healing through the Centuries*, 19.
152   Kydd, *Healing through the Centuries*, 61

The Reliquarial Model of healing promises healing from relics.[153] The Incubational teaches that healing needs nurturing as well as it is progressive and obtained by persevering.[154] The Revelational Model believes that God gives specialized knowledge of what needs are present and verifies who receives healing.[155] The Soteriological Model of healing comes from the perspective that people receive healing miraculously through the same faith that saves them. That is through the atoning work of Jesus.[156] The phrase "healing is in the atonement" is the mantra of this model. This is predominately a Pentecostal model.[157] There is one example of this model presented in the book. That example is the healing ministry of Oral Roberts, who will be discussed later in the book.

This project proposes a mixture of aspects of the two models. The first model will be part of the mix will be the incubational model. In this model, one expects that there would be a time-lapse between prayer and healing. Gradual improvement is acceptable and retains its supernatural status.[158] This model recognizes the help of doctors. Kydd said that powerful preaching was part of this ministry. The second model in this mixture is the soteriological model. In this model, healing is made available by the death, burial, and resurrection of Jesus Christ. One expects healing with the same frequency as receiving forgiveness of sins.

It teaches that when Jesus paid for the forgiveness of sins, He simultaneously purchased the healing of sicknesses. The teaching and preaching keep the person focused on Spirit's work which enhances one's faith that plays a role in receiving healing.

---

153   Kydd, *Healing through the Centuries*, 115.

154   Kydd, *Healing through the Centuries*, 141.

155   Kydd, *Healing through the Centuries*, 167.

156   Kydd, *Healing through the Centuries*, 199.

157   Kydd, *Healing through the Centuries*, 201.

158   Kydd, *Healing through the Centuries*, 146.

The Decline of Divine Healing in the Practice of the Church

There are three causes for the decline of healing in the church: the doctrine of cessationism, the understanding of the sovereignty of God, and the doctrine of suffering. The doctrine of cessationism is the first contributing influence to the decline of divine healing. The Reformers argued that these "signs and wonders" were for a limited time, primarily for the apostolic age. God commissioned the apostles to preach the Gospel, and the miracles were to give credence to their messages. Once the apostles died, there was no need for signs and wonders, including healing.[159] John Calvin was a major proponent of the cessation doctrine. He had two major arguments for the cessation of healing.[160] His first argument is that there is a difference between permanent and temporary signs. Miracles would then serve the temporary purpose of establishing the Gospel message in the first centuries. Due to the establishment of the Gospel, miracles were no longer needed. The Lord's Supper and baptism would replace the miracles. Secondly, human disbelief and ungratefulness were the causes of the cessation of miracles. Calvin gives two forms of evidence for the cessation. The first is historical. The second is experiential.

The second doctrine that may have contributed to the decline of divine healing is the misunderstanding of God's sovereignty. To be sure, God is sovereign. (1 Tim. 6:15) The understanding and application of that fact to theology have been an issue. John Calvin put a limit on eternal salvation and put a limit on the availability of divine

---

159   Douglas Moo, "Divine Healing in the Health and Wealth Gospel," *Trinity Journal* 9, no. 2 (Fall 1988): 194.

160   Pavel Hejzlar, "John Calvin and the Cessation of Miraculous Healing," *Communio Viatorum* 49, no. 1 (2007): 49.

healing.[161] He insisted that individual healing was solely at the discretion of God's Sovereign will for a small group of people. Jonathan Edwards (1703–1758) recognized the tension between healing and Sovereignty. He would teach that there was an interaction between human faith and God's providence.[162]

The third doctrine that may have contributed to the decline of divine healing is the doctrine of suffering. The church believed that a person could more readily identify with Jesus Christ if suffering. Scriptures that referred to suffering now included sickness as part of their interpretation. As a result, every physical healing pericope of the Bible gets reinterpreted to mean healing the inward parts of humanity. Suffering from sickness was now preferred over divine healing. Divine healing was unnecessary and not prominent. Bradley writes about how suffering and martyrdom became proof of the genuine Gospel[163] The Scripture that rose to great prominence was Paul writing to the church of Corinth, "If I have to boast, I will boast of what pertains to my weakness." (2 Cor. 11:30) To the post-Edict of Milan Christians, it was Paul's weakness that was celebrated and not the miracles that worked through him.

The Christian's willingness to suffer and martyrdom was a more prominent defense of Christianity than power displays of the miraculous, according to early literature. Justin Martyr would declare that the Gospel's power was on display in the willingness of the Christians to suffer for their faith. Tertullian says, "Hope in this resurrection amounts to a contempt of death."[164] Ken Blue's details how the church embraced the suffering doctrine. Blue said that when the state stopped persecuting the church, the church had to find a new way to identify with Jesus

---

161   Hejzlar, "John Calvin," 60.

162   King, "A Practical-Theological," 27.

163   Bradley, "Miracles," 73.

164   Bradley, "Miracles," 72.

Christ.[165] The new way of glorifying and identifying with Jesus through suffering became synonymous with sickness. It paved the way for the doctrine of "sanctification through sickness."[166] As a result, the church despised the healing ministry. The church twisted scriptures on divine healing to only apply to the soul. For instance, James 5:13–18, a healing pericope, was used to justify "last rites."[167] They taught that when the verse says the sick person would be well, they were going to heaven, which is the ultimate healing.

An examination of two scriptures that refer to suffering reveals another perspective on what is meant by suffering. In I Peter 4, Peter writes about how Christ suffered and that Christians should prepare themselves to suffer too. Verses one and two suggest that the suffering would include dealing with sin and living submitted to God. Christians are taught not to allow the passions of their flesh to guide them. Sunwoo Hwang wrote that Christians suffered by dealing with their lusts and "make a clear break from them."[168] Philippians 3:10 addresses the subject of suffering in a significant way. Here Paul talks about having ". . . fellowship of His sufferings . . ." What could that mean? Myles Werntz wrote that Christians must resist the concept that suffering includes physical sickness.[169] He states that Paul wrote about the persecutions that Christ, Christians, and he suffered, including specifics like shipwrecks, beatings, and imprisonments but never included diseases or sicknesses.[170] The suffering was always "for the Gospel."[171] To be sure,

---

165   Ken Blue, *Authority to Heal* (Downers Grove, Ill.: InterVarsity Press, 1987), chap. 1, Kindle.

166   Blue, *Authority to Heal*, chap. 1.

167   Blue, *Authority to Heal*, chap. 1.

168   Sunwoo Hwang, "Participation in Christ's Suffering in 1 Peter 4:1-6," 성경과 신학 82 (2017): 137.

169   Myles Werntz, "The Fellowship of Suffering: Reading Philippians with Stanley Hauerwas," *Review & Expositor* 112, no. 1 (February 2015): 144–50, doi:10.1177/0034637314564548, 144.

170   Werntz, "The Fellowship of Suffering," 146.

171   Werntz, "The Fellowship of Suffering," 149.

suffering is part of being a Christian. The Christian should expect to suffer. Christians suffer by resisting sin and flesh. Christian suffering includes dealing with persecution. While the sick suffer, it is not the same as the suffering mentioned in the New Testament that Christians should embrace. In fact, Blue quotes Ulrich Mueller when he contrasted the difference in the way Christians deal with suffering as persecution from the way Christians deal with sickness by saying, "Nowhere do we find the Biblical admonition to tolerate sickness and to come to terms with it."[172]

The Church Rediscovers Divine Healing

Several individuals contributed to the recovery of the doctrine of healing in the modern era. When Azusa Street Revival, the birth of the modern Pentecostal church, exploded worldwide. Charles Parham and William Seymour led this group during the outpouring. Healing in the atonement was one of the doctrines that received significant focus. Seymour said, "a sanctified body is one that is cleansed from all sickness and disease."[173] For many following decades, Pentecostals held to Seymour's view on healing in the atonement. Many individuals were with the Voice of Healing Revival with Oral Roberts, Gordon Lindsay, T. L. Osborn, and Kenneth Hagin.[174] The most prominent of these was Oral Roberts. The divine healing he received at a George Moncey crusade when has seventeen is the beginning of his healing ministry's development.[175] The Lord spoke to him, commissioning him to preach

---

172   Blue, *Authority to Heal*, chap. 1.

173   Synan, "A Healer in the House," 196.

174   Keith Warrington, "The Teaching And Praxis Concerning Supernatural Healing of British Pentecostals, of John Wimber and Kenneth Hagin in the Light of an Analysis of the Healing Ministry of Jesus as Recorded in the Gospels" (Doctor of Philosophy, Kings College, London, 1999), 94, ProQuest Dissertations & Theses Global.

175   Yong Kim, "Increasing Faith Through Teaching About Divine Healing" (Doctor of Ministry, Oral Roberts University, Tulsa, OK, 2006), 72–73, ProQuest Dissertations & Theses Global.

healing and to begin Oral Roberts University. He held more than 300 crusades. Although his ministry and teachings closely aligned with the Pentecostal Holiness Church, some consider him a modern faith leader.[176] He would build a hospital called, The City of Faith that would merge medicine and prayer.[177] His development of concepts like "seed-faith" and "point of contact" comes in direct opposition to the doctrines of cessationism, misunderstanding of the sovereignty of God, and the suffering doctrine.

Roberts would say that present-day miracles are not easily explained and will make massive changes in the people who receive them.[178] Two theological suppositions flanked Oral Roberts' healing ministry. The first is that God is a good God. This supposition intimated that God was predisposed to heal people and prosper them.[179] Within this doctrine of "God is good," there is a belief that healing is wholeness. Specifically, God wants to heal the whole person: spirit, soul, and body. God is so good that He does not just want to heal the physical body but every part of a person's life, including their finances. Included in the belief that God heals because He is good is the revelation that God wants to heal everyone.

He would tell people he prayed for, "Know that God's Will is to heal you." One receives healing by having confidence (faith) in God's goodness, willingness, and ability to heal. A nuance of the faith characterized by Roberts was the teaching on the point of contact. He taught that the point of contact was where your faith connects with God.[180] The second

---

176   King, "Increasing Faith," 51.

177   Synan, "A Healer in the House," 199.

178   Gary W. Derickson, "The Cessation of Healing Miracles in Paul's Ministry," *Bibliotheca Sacra* 155, no. 619 (July 1998): 302.

179   Kydd, *Healing through the Centuries*, 205.

180   Kydd, *Healing through the Centuries*, 206.

theological supposition of Oral Roberts' healing ministry was that God is sovereign. Oral Roberts would seem to go between two poles. One pole of certainty of healing. The second pole of Sovereignty of God. He would maintain a balance between the two and allow for the mystery in the healing ministry.[181]

Roberts wrestled with why some people did not get healed.[182] Roberts believed that when someone did not get healed, God chose not to heal them. He thought that God would have a larger purpose in not healing someone. Kydd said that Roberts just accepted the mystery and kept praying for people to get healed. This gave way to the "now" and "not yet" aspects of the atonement.[183] God paid the way for everyone to get healed. It was potentially available, but believers can only expect to experience a certain amount of freedom here on earth and get fullness in heaven. He would keep one hand on God's sovereignty and the other on the accessibility of healing.

The Modern Church's Relationship With Divine Healing

The modern church is in flux concerning dealing with divine healing. Some parts of the church fully accept the doctrine of divine healing and practice it. While other parts of the church, including parts of the Pentecostal/Charismatic church, oppose the teaching and practice of divine healing.

Those Who Accept the Doctrine and Practice of Divine Healing

---

181   King, "Increasing Faith," 313.

182   Kydd, *Healing through the Centuries*, 209.

183   Kydd, *Healing through the Centuries*, 210.

Some ministries and denominations have healing as a central element of their doctrine. For instance, the Assembly of God has divine healing as a "cardinal doctrine."[184] Trask, former General Superintendent of the Assemblies of God, wrote,

In Mark 2, Jesus healed a man who was lowered through the roof. Jesus said to the man: 'Thy sins be forgiven thee' (verse 5). The scribes and Pharisees murmured in their hearts. Jesus exposed their murmuring and their faultfinding: 'Whether is it easier to say to the sick of the palsy, Thy sins be forgiven thee; or to say, Arise, and take up thy bed, and walk?' (verse 9). The point is: There are not two kinds of faith; there is one faith. The faith a person needs to be saved is the same faith a person needs to be healed.[185]

Current Superintendent Doug Clay wrote, "Christ's death on the cross not only provides for forgiveness of sin but also healing for sickness. The One who gave you the gift of eternal life is the same One who can heal your body."[186] Outside of the AG, there are lesser-known current ministries like Sandra Kennedy of Whole Life Ministries, a graduate of Southwestern Baptist Seminary. She built her ministry upon the foundation of divine healing. Her ministry focus on divine healing is nearly exactly as the one presented in this book. She describes her ministry as being a place where the "Word of God is exalted, the healing power of God is manifested, and to demonstrate the love and compassion of Christ. People come from across the nation and worldwide to learn how to receive their healing by the power of the Word."[187] The operation of her ministry as patients the people who are seeking healing. The

---

184   Thomas Trask, "Defining Truths of the Assemblies of God: Divine Healing," *Enrichment* Q3, (2007): 1.

185   Trask, "Defining Truths," 1.

186   "Assemblies of God (USA) Official Web Site | Divine Healing," Ag.Org., accessed June 10, 2022, https://ag.org/Beliefs/Our-Core-Doctrines/Divine-Healing.

187   "About", Sandra Kennedy Ministries, accessed May 8, 2021, https://www.sandrakennedy.org/about/.

person seeking healing would then be in a program where they would receive many hours of teaching on healing and be encouraged to study the Bible. The infusion of teaching on healing and hearing scriptures strengthens faith enough to receive healing, which is nearly exactly like the prescribed procedure of transmission presented in this book.

Those Who Reject the Doctrine and Practice of Divine Healing

It appears that some churches, even Charismatic churches, have a tenuous relationship with divine healing. There are three places where the modern church is missing the mark. These three issues directly relate to the "teach, preach, and heal" model.

Deemphasis of Preaching and Demonstrating Healing

The first issue is the deemphasis on preaching and demonstration of healing. Modern preachers may find preaching divine healing as something fanatical and strange to a skeptical culture. Their point might be that focusing on divine healing would hinder church growth. Collin Hart countered this when he wrote, "Healing does not hinder but encourage the preaching of the Gospel."[188] Yong Ha Kim's dissertation found that "through the healing education; however, the participants recovered healing power and experienced healing. This became their testimonies, which significantly affect other people."[189] Kim also found that "believers who experienced healing always preach the Gospel to those around them." Furthermore, new believers seemed to generate more new

---

188   Colin Hart, *Receive Healing*, Trans., Kwang Ho Lee (Seoul: Christian Literature Society, 1988), 291.

189   Lee Kim, "Increasing Faith Through Preaching Sermons on Worship in Sunday Morning Sermons" (Doctor of Ministry, Oral Roberts University, Tulsa, OK, 2008), 119, ProQuest Dissertations & Theses Global.

believers. If accepted that churches and congregations deemphasize preaching and teaching healing because of perceived church growth issues, it completely undermines the "teach, preach, and heal" model. Historically, the church has been most effective when it emphasizes the supernatural ministry of the Holy Spirit. Douglas Moo writes that Matthew 9:35 is the foundation of Jesus' model of ministry, which is that He would teach, preach, and heal.[190] He notes that in Jesus' model, He never turns away someone who desires healing. Jesus healed people who came to Him.

Lack of Biblical Literacy

In general, the deemphasis on preaching and teaching will produce a lack of Biblical literacy or a desire for it. The one seeking healing needs to have their faith developed by the Word of God (Rom. 10:17). If that does not happen, then one of the significant components of receiving healing is removed. Since faith comes through the revelation of the Scripture, there is little faith when there is little revelation of the Scripture. The church needs to put a renewed focus on the role of preaching and faith for healing.

The preaching of faith needs to be front and center to help develop the desire and demonstration of divine healing. The church would heed the words of Moravian missionary Peter Bohler who counseled John Wesley, "Preach faith until you have it, and when you have it, preach faith."[191] Kim maintained that preaching the Bible became "spiritual food that brings faith, change in lifestyle and maturity in Christian faith."[192]

---

190   Moo, "Divine Healing," 193.
191   King, "Increasing Faith," 29.
192   Kim, "Increasing Faith," abstract.

Cessationism Challenge

There is a continued push-back on divine healing from cessationists. To combat this, the church needs to be intentional about teaching the continuance of miracles. Randy Clark writes that the church needs to bridge the gap by preaching and teaching more on the continuance doctrine to help skeptics become adherents.[193] Clark maintains that a very poor exegesis of the Scriptures renders the cessation doctrine Biblically bankrupt.[194] Peter Wagner said, "The power that worked in Jesus for His miraculous ministry not only is related to the power available to us today; it is the same."[195] Derickson, who argues for cessation, admits that it is a doctrine founded chiefly on silence and that an "argument from silence never settles a question conclusively."[196] The application of this MRP addresses all three of these issues.

Conclusion of the Historical/Theological Reflection

The "teach, preach, and heal" model can enhance one's divine healing experience. Church history intertwines the preaching of the Gospel with divine healing. It also shows that divine healing has come through various models and methods, each producing testimonies of healing. However, there have been solid theological opponents of divine healing that have led to periods of decline. God had raised equally strong voices that articulated the doctrine and demonstrated the practice of divine healing, similar to the model presented in this book. Thomas Mathew describes what today's NT ministries should look like when he says, "Most contemporary theological writings lack the supernatural aspect of Christian ministry, but a New Testament model of ministry

---

193   Randy Clark, *There is More* (Chosen: Bloomington, Minnesota, 2013), 121.

194   Clark, *There is More*, 123.

195   Derickson, "The Cessation," 301.

196   Derickson, "The Cessation," 305.

embodies Spirit-empowered preaching, teaching, healing, and leading."[197] As the church embodies this ministry model, the result should be that divine healing is more than a doctrinal position of Spirit-filled believers. Instead, it should be a normative experience for all who seek for it.

---

197   Thomas K. Mathew, *Spirit-Led Ministry in the Twenty-First: Spirit-Empowered Preaching, Teaching, Healing, and Leadership* (West Bow Press., 2017), chap. 3, Kindle.

CHAPTER 7

TPH Model Tested and Verified

PROJECT IMPLEMENTATION

Is there a way to enhance a person's experience of divine healing? The project aims to equip believers to use the Christ-centered model of "teach, preach, and heal" (TPH) to obtain an enhanced divine healing experience. The project will work from the directional research hypothesis that believers seeking divine healing and daily reading and/or listening to sermons about divine healing will have their experience with divine healing enhanced measured by elimination of the sickness, decreased symptoms, a perceived increase of faith for divine healing, and an increase of knowledge about divine healing. This is accomplished by studying the Christ-centered model "teach, preach and heal" in Matthew 9:35 within Evangel World Prayer Center in Louisville, KY, and Evangel North Church in Clarksville, IN. This study seeks to determine if this model enhances people's experience with divine healing so believers/churches can use this model to help those seeking divine healing.

Specifically, the project seeks to increase the understanding of the role of the Christ-centered model of teaching, preaching, and healing as it relates to receiving divine healing. This study starts from the premise that God included divine physical healing in the atonement, and it also observes that recovery rates because of divine healing can be improved. The church must explore every possible methodology to help improve divine healing experiences. It would make logical sense for the church to study the topic of healing to execute God's will based on the revelation of the atonement to His people. If there is a Biblical model of receiving the healing transmission more consistently, the church should endeavor to learn about that model and how to apply that model.

Secondly, since, as is the premise of this study, healing is intertwined with salvation as part of the atonement, the church has a responsibility to help people receive healing in the same way it endeavors to help people receive salvation. The Scripture that is the foundation of this study indicates that healing was as integral as the teaching and preaching in the earthly ministry of Jesus to spread the Gospel. Healing was not seen as a side, unnecessary, superfluous activity of Jesus but very important to the ministry of Jesus. His eternal message of salvation and wholeness had a temporal element of peace and healing. In Mark's version of the commission for the church, Jesus relayed a direct expectation that the church would have as part of its ongoing mission to heal the sick. (Mk 16:18) The transmission methodology in this commission is the laying on of hands. This study recognizes that Jesus did not limit the healing ministry to laying hands upon sick people. This project aims to examine a model of receiving divine healing, but it does not assume it will remove all mystery surrounding receiving divine healing.

Why is the Project Important?

This project looks to provide a model for receiving divine healing. The rate at which people receive divine healing is meager compared to what is perceived from Scripture but high enough to be taken seriously as a divine act. If, as established in the Biblical reflection part of this project, healing is in the atonement, then it is not overstating that recovery is a weighty issue to God as He seeks to remedy the suffering of humanity. If divine healing is important to God, it should go without saying that healing should be important to the church today. It is improper to evaluate the truth of the low recovery rate of those seeking divine healing as not worth continuing to explore possible methods to enhance people's healing experience. If God has given humanity the information through the life and ministry of Jesus as to how to receive divine healing, it will behoove the church to study it further.

This project is important now because people are hurting and need help in receiving divine healing. Even as this proposal is being written, the world is still reeling from a global pandemic, COVID-19. The church can provide additional tools to tap into God's sovereign healing power to help curb this pandemic. This project demonstrates that the church can help people deal with this pandemic and all other sicknesses and diseases.

This project proposes that the church can become better equipped to help people receive divine healing, and as a result, it will also help the church increase its effectiveness in evangelism. When people get healed at a significant rate, it is assumed that they will become more receptive to the message of the Gospel of Jesus Christ. This makes this project of paramount importance.

The Project Strategy

The strategy of this project will be defined in three areas. First, the number of participants. Secondly, the scope of time of the project. Thirdly, the content of the project.

The Participants

The number of participants is affected by numerous factors. Most of those factors are not controllable because they will be volunteer based. This project will limit the number of participants to fifty. The participants will be divided into two groups. The first group will be the control group. The second group will be the test group. They will come from a pool of volunteers from Evangel World Prayer Center and Evangel North Church. The combined size of these congregations is more than 1,000 people.

Church members will be asked to volunteer to participate in this project. For two weeks, applications will be received from those interested in participating in the project. It will be announced in the church services, and information will be in the bulletin.

It will not be advertised online because this project is limited to working only within the church. The participants will be divided into two groups (control and test) and will be randomly selected from those who apply for the project. They will be informed that this is a doctoral project for ORU. The participants will be informed that they will be divided into two groups.

The Control Group

The control group will be asked to do very little. First, they will complete the pretest questionnaire. They will then continue as they have previously. This would include church attendance, prayer, Bible reading, and whatever else makes up their spiritual life. At the end of the 21 days, they will be asked to do a post-test questionnaire.

The Test Group

The test group will be asked to do more than the control group. First, they will be notified that they are selected for the test group. They will be asked to meet on a Sunday evening with the date to be determined. Like the control group, they will be asked to complete the pretest questionnaire. At the end of the 21 days, they will be asked to complete a post-test questionnaire. However, during the 21 days, they will be asked to listen to sermons daily and read Scriptures concerning healing in addition to their normal spiritual life activities. The difference between the control and test groups is the concentrated environment of teaching and preaching done daily for 21 days.

The Scope of Time

Time is an essential aspect of this project. The duration of the project is three weeks. Arguably, this amount of time is sufficient to help people receive a concentration on teaching and preaching. However, it is not too long that will cause people to drop out due to the inability to focus on a very long project. Some people are projected only to complete part of the three weeks. Another aspect of time deals with what is expected to be done daily.

The test group will be expected to watch, with minimal distraction, a sermon presented by the researcher every day. Throughout the day, they will be expected to read and meditate on a list of Scriptures that deal specifically with healing and develop their own list that might be more customized to their specific situation. Additional sermons will be recommended as the participant has the margin for it during their day. The participants are expected to spend time in prayer each day, with some of that time directed toward asking for healing.

The Content of the Project

The concentrated teaching environment will have several specific features. First, the test group will meet in person on a Sunday evening. This meeting will not count toward the 21 days. The purpose of the meeting will be to explain what will be asked of them for the duration of the project.

They will have already been informed of the expectations of the project. It is entirely possible that some may refuse to continue when they realize what is expected of them. They will meet for three more Sunday evenings. In the proceeding days (Monday through Saturday), they will be asked to listen to specific sermons by John Carmichael via Right Now Media. They will be given outlines for all the sermons for the twenty-one days.

The project's content is multifaceted, uses technology, and considers some restrictions that might remain because of COVID-19, namely masks and social distance. There will be an application, a pre-questionnaire, and a post-questionnaire. The participants will meet on four consecutive Sundays. The first Sunday will be an introductory meeting. The next three weeks will involve watching a sermon via Right Now Media, Monday through Saturday, including teaching, Scripture reading, and prayer. On Sundays, they will attend a one-hour healing service at Evangel North Church that includes teaching and prayer.

The In-Person Meeting

There will be a total of four in-person meetings. The meetings will occur on Sunday nights at 6 PM in the sanctuary of Evangel North Church. The meeting will last roughly one hour.

Right Now Media

Right Now Media is a media partner with Evangel World Prayer Center. The participants can use their phones, tablets, or computers to engage with the material. There will be twenty-one sessions. Each session will have a video of the teaching, a document of the outlines of the teachings that can be downloaded or printed, and a place for responses or questions. The participants will receive an invitation to the sessions on Right Now Media. They will be given the phone number of the researcher if they have any technical issues.

The Sermons

The sermons are at the core of the project. There are twenty-one sermons. The sermons cover a wide range of topics concerning enhancing one's experience with divine healing. Some are topical sermons. Others are expository sermons. They will range from Biblical sermons to more theological sermons. Each sermon starts with Scripture. There is an interrogative aspect of each sermon. This reveals the question the sermon addresses. The sermon outlines are part of the material the participant can download and print. This project does not specifically differentiate between which sermon is a teaching sermon or a preaching sermon. This project works from the point of view that the sermons contain both teaching and preaching.

The Analysis

The information from the tests will provide insight into the effectiveness of teaching, preaching, and healing methodology. The question to be answered is whether listening to teaching and preaching on a daily basis enhanced their experience with divine healing. The control pretest and post-test numbers will be compared to the pretest and post-test numbers of the test group. The analysis will focus on five areas. The first area is the age of the participant. The second area is the completeness of the program. The third is physical symptoms. The fourth is the spiritual area. The fifth is the intellectual area.

Age Analysis

The first area this project will analyze is the age of the participant. Age is believed to have affected the recovery of many sicknesses. The young appear to recover faster than those who are older. Age may also play a role in being able to understand the messages. For example, it may be discovered that the older participants could connect to the teaching content more than the younger participants. It may also be discovered that the older do not complete the program due to the transmission by use of the technology employed by this project. The content receptibility and the level of completeness might be related to the participant's age.

Completeness of the Program Analysis

The second area this project will analyze is how much of the program the participants completed. It is suspected that some will not complete the program. The percentage of completeness will be used to evaluate for changes in symptoms, faith, and knowledge if any changes occur. For example, those who complete fifty percent of the program will report changes in their experience from a physical, spiritual, and intellectual perspective. Those results will be compared with those who complete one hundred percent of the program.

Physical Symptoms Analysis

The third area this project will analyze is the severity of physical symptoms to measure the enhancement of a person's divine healing experience. This analysis will involve self-reporting of the severity of symptoms. The participants will be asked to self-report the level of the symptoms in the pretest. At the end of the post-test, the participants will be asked to self-report total healing or complete alleviation of symptoms. If symptoms remain but have changed, they will be asked to select from a range of changes. The participants will also be able to report that there is no change in symptoms or even that the symptoms have worsened. This project does not ask for medical records; therefore, it depends entirely on the participants' self-reporting.

Spiritual Analysis

The fourth area this project will analyze is the spiritual enhancement of their experience with divine healing. This will be measured by the participant self-reporting changes in two aspects of their spiritual life. The first is their faith for divine healing. The second is their perception of their closeness with God. The participants will be asked to select if their faith has lessened, stayed the same, grown somewhat, or grown significantly. The participant will be asked to select if their closeness with God has lessened, stayed the same, grown somewhat, or grown significantly.

Intellectual Analysis

The fifth area this project will analyze is the intellectual area of enhancement of their experience with divine healing. The participants will be asked to self-report their knowledge of divine healing. They will be exposed to twenty-one messages that deal directly or indirectly with divine healing. The participants will be asked if they believe their knowledge has lessened, stayed the same, grown somewhat, or grown significantly.

The Limitations

There are several limitations of the project. This project entirely depends on the willingness of the members of EWPC and ENC to apply to participate in the project. Some might be reluctant to share the information with the researcher leading this project even though their names will be withheld. Some might be reluctant because the four in-person meetings will be held at ENC. ENC is in Southern Indiana. Several participants are suspected to be from EWPC in Louisville, KY. This means that the participants must cross over one of the toll bridges. This might prove to be a hindrance for some people. It is one thing to start the project.

It is another thing to complete the project. As stated, 21 days is a reasonable timeframe. The question is, is it long enough to get an accurate recovery measurement? Another question is whether the participants can stay focused for three weeks. For some people, it may prove to be too long of time.

Expected Project Outcome

The expected outcome of this project is a teaching manual that churches can use to help enhance people's experience with divine healing. This enhancement will include alleviating symptoms, growing their faith, and increasing their knowledge about divine healing.

This manual will become an easy-to-use resource that will help ministers and the people seeking healing to become more intentional about receiving divine healing. Again, this will not take all the mystery out of divine healing, but it will help the church use the clues about divine healing that God has provided to humanity through the life and ministry of Jesus.

The Population

The study population was recruited from Evangel World Prayer Center and Evangel North Church. Recruiting began Tuesday, September 26, after approval from IRB. The recruiting efforts included having people talk to, call, text, or email the student researcher if they were interested in participating in the study. Those who contacted the student researcher were informed of the purpose and duration of the study. They were emailed an application and consent form. Those who returned the completed application and consent form were randomly placed in either the control or test group. On Friday, October 6, they were notified of which group they were placed in and sent an email with specific instructions. Ninety-six people contacted the student researcher to say they were interested in the study. Of those interested in the study, 61 returned a completed application and consent form. Due to the method of randomization (app that chose either test or control), there were 35 in the test group and 26 in the control group. The test group saw 33 complete the pre-study questionnaire and 32 complete the post-study questionnaire. This reveals that one participant dropped out of the test group during the study. The control group saw 21 complete the pre-study questionnaire and 14 complete the post-study questionnaire. This reveals that seven participants from the control group dropped out of the study. Although they were not asked, many participants informed the student researcher about their illnesses. The illnesses ranged from cosmetic to life-threatening.

The Content

The test group and the control group had different instructions for the study. The test group watched 21 sermons presented by the study researcher. They were instructed to listen to the sermons as often as possible with the goal of at least once a day. They were also instructed to listen to sermons by other ministers as often as possible. Additionally, they were to daily read through a list of healing scriptures provided by the student researcher. The sermons were a combination of expository and topical sermons that covered a wide range of theological and Biblical concepts. All of the sermons were meant to inspire and inform the participants concerning divine healing. The topics covered included explaining the teach, preach, and heal methodology in Matthew 4:23 and 9:35, healing in the atonement, the role of faith, and inspirational messages concerning several healing narratives. The feedback from the participants was very optimistic concerning the content of the sermons. It is likely that some of the participants had negative feedback to give but chose to withhold it. The control group was not given access to the material or the in-person meetings.

The study ran smoothly. Initially, a few participants needed help setting up the Right Now Media account. Most of the participants could access Right Now Media with no trouble. One participant could not access it, so they were given special access to the videos through YouTube. The videos were hidden from the public. Some participants in the control group expressed disappointment at not being given access to the material even though they were told they would be given access after the study concluded. This might explain why there were several dropouts in the control group.

Results

The study's results mainly focus on the post-study questionnaire, although the pre-study questionnaire provides some background of the participants. The pre-study categories are age of participants, frequency of Bible reading, symptom level, faith in divine healing, closeness to God, and knowledge about divine healing. The categories analyzed for the post-study are as follows: age, level of completeness, self-reported change of symptoms, changes in faith for divine healing, changes in a perceived closeness to God, and changes in knowledge of divine healing.

Pre-Study for Test and Control Groups

Table 1 shows the age of the participants for both the test and control groups from the pre-study questionnaire. The average age of the participants is 59 for both groups. The fact that the average age for both groups is identical removes the possibility that age is a factor in why one group had a different result from the other group.

Table 1. Age of Participants in Test and Control Pre-Study

Age	Test	Control
18–29	1	0
30–49	6	2
50–69	17	15
70+	9	4
Total Participants	33	21
Average Age	59	59

Table 2 shows the Bible reading frequency in the test and control groups from the pre-study questionnaire. In the test group, 23 participants read the Bible daily, and 10 read the Bible weekly. In the control group, 15 participants read the Bible daily, and six read the Bible weekly. When looking at the percentages, these groups are nearly identical, with the test group at 70% daily and 30% weekly, while the control group is at 71% daily and 29% weekly.

Table 2. Frequency of Reading the Bible in Test and Control Pre-Study

Frequency	Test	Control
Daily	23	15
Weekly	10	6
Total Participants	33	21

Table 3 shows the results of the symptom level of the test group and the control group pre-study questionnaires. The levels are defined as follows: 0–3 means a low symptom level in their current malady(ies); 4–6 means an average experience of symptoms in their current malady(ies); 7–10 indicates a high level of symptoms in their current malady(ies). The test group averaged 6.91, and the control group averaged 6.81. The test and control groups had a comparable percentage of high symptom levels at 61% and 66%, respectively. However, the control group only had 5% at a low level of symptoms, while the test group had 18% at a low symptom level. On average the test group scored themselves slightly higher than the control group.

Table 3. Symptom Level in Test and Control Pre-Study

Symptom Level in Test and Control Pre-Study		
Symptom Level	Test	Control
0–3	6	1
4–6	7	6
7–10	20	14
Total	33	21
Average	6.91	6.81

Table 4 shows the perceived faith level in divine healing from the test and the control group's pre-study questionnaire. This is the first aspect of the spiritual analysis of the study. Both groups were told that this project is seeking to measure their faith to be healed of their current malady.

A zero indicates no faith to be healed. A ten indicates the participant perceives they have a high level of faith to be healed of their malady. The control group had a very high faith in divine healing at 95% in the highest levels, while the test group had 72% in the highest levels. The test group had more people in the middle level of faith in divine healing at 24%, while the control group was at zero. The control group was overall at a higher level of faith than the test group.

Table 4. Faith for Healing in Test and Control Pre-Study

Faith Level	Test	Control
0–3	1	1
4–6	8	0
7–10	24	20
Total	33	21
Average	7.88	8.86

Table 5 reveals the results of the pre-study questionnaire for the test and control in the category of perceived closeness to God. This is the second aspect of the spiritual analysis of enhancing their experience with divine healing.

The test group scored slightly lower than the control group with an average of 7.61 compared to 7.90. This puts both groups on the same level.

Table 5. Closeness to God in Test and Control Pre-Study

Closeness Level	Test	Control
0–3	2	1
4–6	5	4
7–10	26	16
Total	33	21
Average	7.61	7.90

Table 6 shows the perceived knowledge of divine healing from the test and control group's pre-study questionnaire. The control group had a higher level of knowledge about divine healing at an average of 7.81 compared to the test group at 6.91.

Table 6. Knowledge of Divine Healing in Test and Control Pre-Study

Knowledge Level	Test	Control
0–3	4	0
4–6	10	7
7–10	19	14
Total	33	21
Average	6.91	7.81

Post-Study Age of Test and Control Groups

Table 7 shows the age of the participants for both the test and control groups from the post-study questionnaire. The average age of the participants is 59 for the test group and 62 for the control group. The control group was slightly older than the test group.

Table 7. Age of Participants in Test and Control Post-Study

Age of Participants	Test	Control
18–29	1	0
30–49	5	1
50–69	18	9
70+	8	4
Total Participants	32	14
Average Age	59	62

Post-Study Level of Completeness of Test Group

Table 8 shows the level of completeness of the 21 sermons the test group participants completed as reported on the post-study questionnaire. All of the test group participants listened to some of the sermons. Over 80% of the participants completed most or all of the study material. When a 4.0 scale is applied (All=4, Most=3, Half=2, Few=1, None=0), the group scored an average of 3.31. As a whole, the test group completed most or all of the study materials.

Table 8. Completion Level in Test Group Post-Study

Completion Level	Number of Participants	Percentage
None	0	0%
Few	2	6%
Half	3	9%
Most	10	31%
All	17	53%
Total	32	100%
Average	3.31	

Post-Study Self-Reported Change in Symptoms for Test and Control Groups

Table 9 shows the self-reported symptom improvement from the post-study questionnaire from both the test and control groups. Over 87% of the test group experienced symptom improvement, while over 35% of the control group saw improvement. Nearly 60% of the test group experienced 50% or better symptom improvement, while just over 7% of the control group experienced 50% or better symptom improvement. The average improvement of the test group was over 47% compared to the average improvement of the control group, which was nearly 13%, also shown in Figure 1.

Table 9. Test vs Control Post-Study Percent of Symptom Improvement

Percentage Improvement	Test Group	Control Group
100%	6.25%	0.00%
75%	31.25%	7.14%
50%	21.88%	0.00%
25%	28.13%	28.57%
0%	12.50%	64.29%
Any Improvement	87.50%	35.71%
50% or Better	59.38%	7.14%
Average Improvement	47.66%	12.50%

Figure 1. Summary Chart of Symptom Improvement of Test vs Control Group

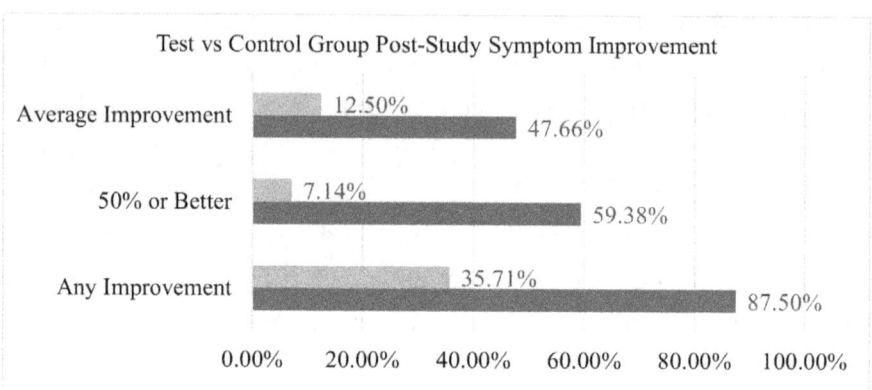

Post-Study Changes in Faith for Divine Healing for Test and Control Groups

Table 10 shows the post-study change in faith in both groups. The test group experienced a significant increase in faith in divine healing. The control group largely remained the same.

Table 10. Change in Faith in Both Groups Post-Study

Faith Change	Test	Control
Lessened	0.00%	0.00%
Same	6.25%	71.43%
Somewhat	18.75%	14.29%
Significantly	75.00%	14.29%
Total	100.00%	100.00%

Post-Study Changes in a Perceived Closeness to God for Test and Control Groups

Table 11 shows both groups' post-study changes in closeness with God. Both groups experienced an increase in their perceived closeness with God. In the test group, 93.75% experienced an increase. In the control group, 57.14% experienced an increase.

Table 11. Change in Closeness with God in Both Groups Post-Study

Closeness Change	Test	Control
Lessened	0.00%	0.00%
Same	6.25%	42.86%
Somewhat	25.00%	50.00%
Significantly	68.75%	7.14%
Total	100.00%	100.00%

Post-Study Changes in Knowledge of Divine Healing for Test and Control Groups

Table 12 shows changes in both groups' post-study knowledge of divine healing. In the test group, 93.76% experienced an increase. In the control group, 35.71% experienced an increase.

Table 12. Change in Knowledge of Divine Healing in Both Groups Post-Study

Knowledge Change	Test	Control
Lessened	0.00%	0.00%
Same	6.25%	64.29%
Somewhat	21.88%	28.57%
Significantly	71.88%	7.14%
Total	100.00%	100.00%

The Relationship Between the Participant's Completion Level of the Study Material and Symptom Relief for the Test Group Post-Study

Table 13 shows the relationship between the level of completion and symptom improvement for the test group. Of those who completed all or most of the study, 37.50% experienced 75% to 100% relief from symptoms. Over 50% of the participants who completed all or most of the study experienced 50% to 100% relief from symptoms. Only 15.64% of those in the test group who finished half or less of the study experienced relief from symptoms. Also, only 6.25% of those who completed most or all of the study did not experience symptom reduction.

Table 13. Level of Completion Effect on the Symptom Improvement in Test Group

Symptom Improvement	All	Most	Half	Few	None
100%	0.00%	6.25%	0.00%	0.00%	0.00%
75%	28.13%	3.13%	0.00%	0.00%	0.00%
50%	9.38%	6.25%	6.25%	0.00%	0.00%
25%	12.50%	12.50%	0.00%	3.13%	0.00%
0%	3.13%	3.13%	3.13%	3.13%	0.00%
	All or Most				
75% or Better	37.50%				
50% or Better	53.13%				
0%	6.25%				

Table 14 demonstrates the relationship between completing most or all of the study and its effect on faith in divine healing, closeness with God, and knowledge of divine healing in the test group. In all three categories, there were significant increases. Only 12.51% of the participants who completed most or all of the study did not experience an increase in the three categories.

Table 14. Most or All of the Level of Completion Effect on Three Categories

Categories	Significantly	Somewhat	Same	None
Faith	65.63%	12.50%	6.25%	0.00%
Closeness	62.50%	18.75%	3.13%	0.00%
Knowledge	68.75%	12.50%	3.13%	0.00%

Results To Desired Outcome

The desired outcome was that people who listened to messages about divine healing would have an enhanced divine healing experience. The results of the study confirm that this is the case. The test group had decreased symptoms due to listening to the material compared to the control group. The test group also experienced increased faith in divine healing, perceived closeness to God, and knowledge about divine healing compared to the control group.

Figure 2 shows that within the test group, there was a corresponding increase in reduced symptoms, faith in healing, closeness with God, and knowledge of divine healing for those who completed more of the daily exercises than for those who completed less of the daily exercises.

Figure 2. The Effect of Completeness Level in Four Categories

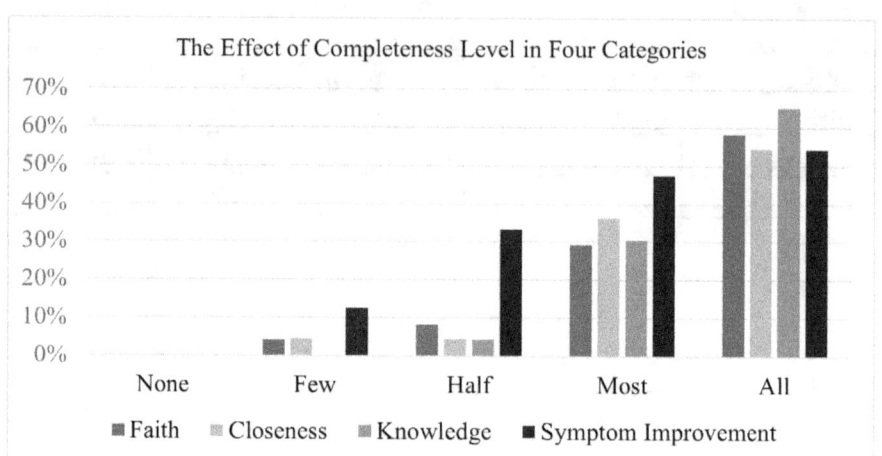

Testimonies

There were several testimonies given. The student researcher did not require the participants to provide testimony. The groups were told their names would not be revealed in the MRP. One woman experienced a 75% reduction in the need for medication for her diabetic condition. Another participant was cured of stage three cancer, verified by a blood test in the last week of the study. A male participant experienced a macular degeneration reversal, confirmed by his ophthalmologist the week after the study. One lady with rheumatoid arthritis who had to take pain medicine every day for the last 11 years testified that in the last five days of the study, there was no pain and no need to take pain medicine. Another person experienced total healing of an injured toe that had not healed in ten months and was told to amputate the toe by her doctor. She sent before and after pictures. It is amazing. One man who had been on heart medication for over 15 years, was told after the study that he no longer needed heart medication. The man showed the student researcher the report. He was in tears as he was sharing this testimony.

CHAPTER 8

21 Days of Healing Sermon Outlines

The focus of this study centers around hearing sermons about divine healing. The following pages contain the outlines of these sermons. They were made available to the participants in the test group.

The content authored by Dr. John Carmichael is owned by Carmichael Ministries, which holds copyright in all of his published works. You may freely use, share, and reproduce this content for personal or non-commercial (not sell or monetize) uses, provided that when publishing textual content online or in hard copy, only quotes and excerpts may be used, not the entire work.

21 DAYS OF HEALING
PASTOR JOHN CARMICHAEL
SESSION 1

Message Title: Receive Healing.

[Mat 4:23 NASB95] 23 Jesus was going throughout all Galilee, teaching in their synagogues and proclaiming the gospel of the kingdom, and healing every kind of disease and every kind of sickness among the people.

[Mat 9:35-36 NASB95] 35 Jesus was going through all the cities and villages, teaching in their synagogues and proclaiming the gospel of the kingdom, and healing every kind of disease and every kind of sickness. 36 Seeing the people, He felt compassion for them, because they were distressed and dispirited like sheep without a shepherd.

INTRODUCTION:

- Jesus' earthly ministry has three facets: teach, preach, and heal.
- "Other than your Sunday and Wednesday messages, I want you to study nothing but healing." January 2006 in Clinton, KY. I was not sick. I already believed in healing.
- Whether you believe COVID-19 is one of the end-time plagues or not, they are coming. We must know how to receive healing.

Interrogative: What should you know right now to receive healing?

Transitional: You need to know two things right now to receive healing.

BODY:

I.   It is God's Will for you to receive healing.

A. HE DECLARED THAT HE WANTS YOU TO RECEIVE HEALING.

1. OT – [Exo 15:26 NASB95] 26 And He said, "If you will give earnest heed to the voice of the LORD your God, and do what is right in His sight, and give ear to His commandments, and keep all His statutes, I will put none of the diseases on you which I have put on the Egyptians; for I, the LORD, am your healer."

2. NT – [Jas 5:14-15 NASB95] 14 Is anyone among you sick? [Then] he must call for the elders of the church and they are to pray over him, anointing him with oil in the name of the Lord; 15 and the prayer offered in faith will restore the one who is sick, and the Lord will raise him up, and if he has committed sins, they will be forgiven him.

B. THE ATONEMENT ITSELF SHOWS IT IS HIS WILL FOR YOU TO RECEIVE HEALING.

1. [Isa 53:4-5 NASB95] 4 Surely our griefs He Himself bore, And our sorrows He carried; Yet we ourselves esteemed Him stricken, Smitten of God, and afflicted. 5 But He was pierced through for our transgressions, He was crushed for our iniquities; The chastening for our well-being [fell] upon Him, And by His scourging we are healed.

2. [Mat 8:16-17 NASB95] 16 When evening came, they brought to Him many who were demon-possessed; and He cast out the spirits with a word, and healed all who were ill. 17 [This was] to fulfill

what was spoken through Isaiah the prophet: "HE HIMSELF TOOK OUR INFIRMITIES AND CARRIED AWAY OUR DISEASES."

C. ONE OF THE MOST CRITICAL STEPS TOWARD RECEIVING HEALING IS TO KNOW IT'S GOD'S WILL FOR YOU TO RECEIVE HEALING.

II. There are many ways for you to receive healing.

A.   THERE HAS ALWAYS BEEN MORE THAN ONE WAY FOR PEOPLE TO RECEIVE HEALING.

B.   NOTE: THERE ARE NATURAL THINGS YOU SHOULD DO AS WELL: SLEEP, DRINK WATER, EXERCISE, TAKE MEDICINE, ETC.

C.   HERE ARE SEVERAL WAYS YOU CAN RECEIVE HEALING.

1. Pray for and speak healing. [Mat 9:21 NASB95] 21 for she was saying to herself, "If I only touch His garment, I will get well."

2. Get around people who operate in the gifts of healings. [1Co 12:9, 28 NASB95] 9 to another faith by the same Spirit, and to another gifts of healing by the one Spirit, ... 28 And God has appointed in the church, first apostles, second prophets, third teachers, then miracles, then gifts of healings, helps, administrations, [various] kinds of tongues.

3. Call for people to lay hands on you. [Act 9:17 NASB95] 17 So Ananias departed and entered the house, and after laying his hands on him said, "Brother Saul, the Lord Jesus, who appeared

to you on the road by which you were coming, has sent me so that you may regain your sight and be filled with the Holy Spirit."

4. Feed on God's Word concerning healing. [Pro 4:20-22 NASB95] 20 My son, give attention to my words; Incline your ear to my sayings. 21 Do not let them depart from your sight; Keep them in the midst of your heart. 22 For they are life to those who find them And health to all their body.

5. Be open to unusual ways to receive healing. [Act 19:11-12 NASB95] 11 God was performing extraordinary miracles by the hands of Paul, 12 so that handkerchiefs or aprons were even carried from his body to the sick, and the diseases left them and the evil spirits went out.

6. Take the Lord's Supper. [1Co 11:29-30 NASB95] 29 For he who eats and drinks, eats, and drinks judgment to himself if he does not judge the body rightly. 30 For this reason many among you are weak and sick, and a number sleep.

7. Deal with demons. [Luk 13:10-13 NASB95] 10 And He was teaching in one of the synagogues on the Sabbath. 11 And there was a woman who for eighteen years had had a sickness caused by a spirit; and she was bent double, and could not straighten up at all. 12 When Jesus saw her, He called her over and said to her, "Woman, you are freed from your sickness." 13 And He laid His hands on her; and immediately she was made erect again and [began] glorifying God.

D.   THROUGHOUT CHURCH HISTORY, PEOPLE HAVE RECEIVED HEALING IN NUMEROUS WAYS. HEALING MINISTRIES OFTEN DIFFERED IN DOCTRINE. HOWEVER, THEY ALL GOT RESULTS.

Why? Faith and trust have more to do with healing than perfect doctrine.

CONCLUSION:

- It is God's Will for you to receive healing in many ways.

21 DAYS OF HEALING
PASTOR JOHN CARMICHAEL
SESSION 2

MESSAGE TITLE: JESUS HEALS YOU.

[Act 9:34 NASB95] 34 Peter said to him, "Aeneas, Jesus Christ heals you; get up and make your bed." Immediately he got up.

INTRODUCTION:

- "Other than your Sunday and Wednesday messages, study nothing but healing." The word of God to me January 2006.
- During that time, I realized the difference between real faith in healing and just "kind of" believing in healing.
- God wants us to learn healing doctrine, but more importantly, how to receive healing by faith.
- These two stories have similarities that will teach us how divine physical healing is received.

Interrogative: What can we learn about divine healing from these two stories?

Transitional: Here are three important aspects of divine healing. (Maybe a fourth bonus at the end.)

BODY
(SCRIPTURE, ILLUSTRATION, ARGUMENTATION, APPLICATION):

I.   The conditions surrounding the healings were similar.

A.   [ACT 9:33, 37 NASB95] 33 THERE HE FOUND A MAN NAMED AENEAS, WHO HAD BEEN BEDRIDDEN EIGHT YEARS, FOR HE WAS PARALYZED. ... 37 AND IT HAPPENED AT THAT TIME THAT SHE FELL SICK AND DIED; AND WHEN THEY HAD WASHED HER BODY, THEY LAID IT IN AN UPPER ROOM.

B.   TIME

C.   EFFECT

D.   THESE TWO THINGS MUST BECOME INCONSEQUENTIAL.

E.   E. JESUS IS TOO _____ (EVERYTHING).

II.   The transmission surrounding the healings was similar.

A.   [ACT 9:34, 40 NASB95] 34 PETER SAID TO HIM, "AENEAS, JESUS CHRIST HEALS YOU; GET UP AND MAKE YOUR BED." IMMEDIATELY HE GOT UP. ... 40 BUT PETER SENT THEM ALL OUT AND KNELT DOWN AND PRAYED, AND TURNING TO THE BODY, HE SAID, "TABITHA, ARISE." AND SHE OPENED HER EYES, AND WHEN SHE SAW PETER, SHE SAT UP.

B.   THERE WAS A DECLARATION AND A FOCUS THAT JESUS IS THE SOURCE HEALING.

C. FAITH WAS RELEASED THROUGH ACTION. THEY WERE TOLD TO ACT HEALED.

NOTE: NONE OF THESE ACTS WERE DANGEROUS.

D. [JAS 5:14-15 NASB95] 14 IS ANYONE AMONG YOU SICK? [THEN] HE MUST CALL FOR THE ELDERS OF THE CHURCH AND THEY ARE TO PRAY OVER HIM, ANOINTING HIM WITH OIL IN THE NAME OF THE LORD; 15 AND THE PRAYER OFFERED IN FAITH WILL RESTORE THE ONE WHO IS SICK, AND THE LORD WILL RAISE HIM UP, AND IF HE HAS COMMITTED SINS, THEY WILL BE FORGIVEN HIM.

E. THIS IS NOT A TIME TO PRAY, "IF IT BE THY WILL." WHY? THE WILL OF GOD IS KNOWN CONCERNING HEALING.

1. Word of God - [Pro 4:20-22 NASB95] 20 My son, give attention to my words; Incline your ear to my sayings. 21 Do not let them depart from your sight; Keep them in the midst of your heart. 22 For they are life to those who find them And health to all their body.

2. Jesus – He is the embodiment of the Will of God. [Act 10:38 NASB95] 38 "[You know of] Jesus of Nazareth, how God anointed Him with the Holy Spirit and with power, and [how] He went about doing good and healing all who were oppressed by the devil, for God was with Him.

3. Atonement

a. [Isa 53:4-5 NASB95] 4 Surely our griefs He Himself bore, And our sorrows He carried; Yet we ourselves esteemed Him stricken, Smitten of God, and afflicted. 5 But He was pierced through for our transgressions, He was crushed for our iniquities; The chastening for our well-being [fell] upon Him, And by His scourging we are healed.

b. [Mat 8:16-17 NASB95] 16 When evening came, they brought to Him many who were demon-possessed; and He cast out the spirits with a word, and healed all who were ill. 17 [This was] to fulfill what was spoken through Isaiah the prophet: "HE HIMSELF TOOK OUR INFIRMITIES AND CARRIED AWAY OUR DISEASES."

F.   F. FAITH BEGINS WHERE THE WILL OF GOD IS KNOWN. [1Jo 5:14-15 NASB95] 14 THIS IS THE CONFIDENCE WHICH WE HAVE BEFORE HIM, THAT, IF WE ASK ANYTHING ACCORDING TO HIS WILL, HE HEARS US. 15 AND IF WE KNOW THAT HE HEARS US [IN] WHATEVER WE ASK, WE KNOW THAT WE HAVE THE REQUESTS WHICH WE HAVE ASKED FROM HIM.

G.   G. WHY IS EVERYONE NOT HEALED? IS GOD'S WILL ALWAYS DONE? DO YOU EVER NOT ACT LIKE JESUS?

III. The conclusion after the healing was similar.

A.   [ACT 9:34-35 NASB95] 34 PETER SAID TO HIM, "AENEAS, JESUS CHRIST HEALS YOU; GET UP AND MAKE YOUR BED." IMMEDIATELY HE GOT UP. 35 AND ALL WHO LIVED AT LYDDA AND SHARON SAW HIM, AND THEY TURNED TO THE LORD.

B.   [ACT 9:40-43 NASB95] 40 BUT PETER SENT THEM ALL OUT AND KNELT DOWN AND PRAYED, AND TURNING TO THE BODY, HE SAID, "TABITHA, ARISE." AND SHE OPENED HER EYES, AND WHEN SHE SAW PETER, SHE SAT UP. 41 AND HE GAVE HER HIS HAND AND RAISED HER UP; AND CALLING THE SAINTS AND WIDOWS, HE PRESENTED HER ALIVE. 42 IT BECAME KNOWN ALL OVER JOPPA,

AND MANY BELIEVED IN THE LORD. 43 AND PETER STAYED MANY
DAYS IN JOPPA WITH A TANNER [NAMED] SIMON.

C.   HEALING OCCURRED. BELIEVE THAT YOU WILL RECEIVE
YOUR HEALING.

D.   FAITH WAS INCREASED. BOTH IN THE PERSON AND
THOSE WHO HEARD ABOUT IT. (NOTE: ONE WAY TO HELP YOUR
FAITH IS TO LISTEN TO THE HEALING TESTIMONIES OF OTHERS.)

E.   WHATEVER LEVEL OF HEALING HAS OCCURRED, LET
IT SPUR YOUR FAITH ONWARD. WHERE ARE THE "SIZE OF A MAN'S
HAND" KIND OF FAITH PEOPLE? [1KI 18:44-46 NASB95] 44 IT
CAME ABOUT AT THE SEVENTH [TIME,] THAT HE SAID, "BEHOLD, A
CLOUD AS SMALL AS A MAN'S HAND IS COMING UP FROM THE SEA."
AND HE SAID, "GO UP, SAY TO AHAB, 'PREPARE [YOUR CHARIOT]
AND GO DOWN, SO THAT THE [HEAVY] SHOWER DOES NOT STOP
YOU.'" 45 IN A LITTLE WHILE THE SKY GREW BLACK WITH CLOUDS
AND WIND, AND THERE WAS A HEAVY SHOWER. AND AHAB RODE
AND WENT TO JEZREEL. 46 THEN THE HAND OF THE LORD WAS
ON ELIJAH, AND HE GIRDED UP HIS LOINS AND OUTRAN AHAB TO
JEZREEL.

CONCLUSION:

- This could be a 4th point: In both cases, sickness and
  disease were unacceptable. There was a desire to challenge the sickness. This is imperative to receive healing.
- Jesus heals you regardless of how long or bad your condition is as you look to Jesus as the source of the transmission of healing while expecting healing to occur and
  faith to be increased.

21 DAYS OF HEALING
PASTOR JOHN CARMICHAEL
SESSION 3
MESSAGE TITLE: FAITH FOR WHOLENESS THROUGH PREACH-
ING.

[Act 14:7-10 NASB95] 7 and there they continued to preach the gospel. 8 At Lystra a man was sitting who had no strength in his feet, lame from his mother's womb, who had never walked. 9 This man was listening to Paul as he spoke, who, when he had fixed his gaze on him and had seen that he had faith to be made well, 10 said with a loud voice, "Stand upright on your feet." And he leaped up and [began] to walk.

INTRODUCTION:

• New studies show that most people believe that our country is headed in a wrong direction. Yet many people in their lives know that they themselves are not exactly what they should be.

• The reality is that God has more for us than we're walking in today. Yet, we need to learn how to tap into God's best for our lives.

• And v14, we see a story of a man who is lame. This story of this healing becomes central to much of what happens in this chapter. Yet we learn some very important principles about how that God brings wholeness into our lives through faith.

Interrogative: How can we have faith that brings wholeness in our lives?

Transitional: Three principles from Acts 14 show us how to develop faith that brings wholeness to our lives.

BODY:

I. God wants us to understand the real condition we are in today.

A. [ACT 14:8 NASB95] 8 AT LYSTRA A MAN WAS SITTING WHO HAD NO STRENGTH IN HIS FEET, LAME FROM HIS MOTHER'S WOMB, WHO HAD NEVER WALKED.

B. THIS VERSE DESCRIBES IN ALMOST REPETITIVE DETAIL THE CONDITION OF THE MAN.

C. TOO MANY TIMES, WE THINK WE ARE "OK," OR WE HAVE ACCEPTED OUR CONDITION WITHOUT REALIZING JUST HOW BAD IT IS.

D. REPENTANCE DOESN'T COME UNTIL WE KNOW THAT WE NEED IT. WE ARE NOT TO BE IN A PLACE OF SELF LOATHING. WE JUST NEED TO UNDERSTAND THAT WE ARE LESS THAN OPTIMAL.

E. UNTIL WE GET TIRED OF OUR CONDITION AND SEE IT AS IT REALLY IS, WE WILL NOT PURSUE SOMETHING BETTER.

F. PEOPLE WHO PURSUE GOD ARE THOSE WHO REALIZE THEIR ABSOLUTE NEED OF HIM.

II. God uses preaching to ignite faith that connects us to wholeness and effectiveness.

A. [ACT 14:7, 9, 21 NASB95] 7 AND THERE THEY CONTINUED TO PREACH THE GOSPEL. ... 9 THIS MAN WAS LISTENING

TO PAUL AS HE SPOKE, WHO, WHEN HE HAD FIXED HIS GAZE ON HIM AND HAD SEEN THAT HE HAD FAITH TO BE MADE WELL, ... 21 AFTER THEY HAD PREACHED THE GOSPEL TO THAT CITY AND HAD MADE MANY DISCIPLES, THEY RETURNED TO LYSTRA AND TO ICONIUM AND TO ANTIOCH

B.   NOTICE: "FAITH TO BE MADE WELL"... IT WAS FAITH FOR TOTAL WHOLENESS. IT WAS FOR SOMETHING. YES, HE LIKELY HAD FAITH IN JESUS, YET IT WAS FOR SOMETHING.

1.   [Heb 11:6 NASB95] 6 And without faith it is impossible to please [Him,] for he who comes to God must believe that He is and [that] He is a rewarder of those who seek Him.

2.   Faith in God's existence and for His reward.

C.   HOW DOES THAT FAITH COME? PREACHING.

1.   [Rom 10:16-17 NASB95] 16 However, they did not all heed the good news; for Isaiah says, "LORD, WHO HAS BELIEVED OUR REPORT?" 17 So faith [comes] from hearing, and hearing by the word of Christ.

D.   THE MAN LISTENED TO PREACHING. FAITH CAME FOR HEALING.

III. God will ask us to act on that faith continually.

A.   [ACT 14:10, 21-23 NASB95] 10 SAID WITH A LOUD VOICE, "STAND UPRIGHT ON YOUR FEET." AND HE LEAPED UP AND [BEGAN] TO WALK. ... 21 AFTER THEY HAD PREACHED THE GOSPEL TO THAT CITY AND HAD MADE MANY DISCIPLES, THEY RETURNED

TO LYSTRA AND TO ICONIUM AND TO ANTIOCH, 22 STRENGTH-
ENING THE SOULS OF THE DISCIPLES, ENCOURAGING THEM TO
CONTINUE IN THE FAITH, AND [SAYING,] "THROUGH MANY TRIBU-
LATIONS WE MUST ENTER THE KINGDOM OF GOD." 23 WHEN THEY
HAD APPOINTED ELDERS FOR THEM IN EVERY CHURCH, HAVING
PRAYED WITH FASTING, THEY COMMENDED THEM TO THE LORD IN
WHOM THEY HAD BELIEVED.

B.   IN THIS CHAPTER, WE SEE TWO THINGS ABOUT FAITH:

1. Action

a. Acts 14:10

b. [Jas 2:22-24, 26 NASB95] 22 You see that faith was working with his works, and as a result of the works, faith was perfected; 23 and the Scripture was fulfilled which says, "AND ABRAHAM BELIEVED GOD, AND IT WAS RECKONED TO HIM AS RIGHTEOUSNESS," and he was called the friend of God. 24 You see that a man is justified by works and not by faith alone. ... 26 For just as the body without [the] spirit is dead, so also faith without works is dead.

2. Endurance

a. Acts 14:21-23 – here established people and churches.

b. [2Ti 3:12 NASB95] 12 Indeed, all who desire to live godly in Christ Jesus will be persecuted.

CONCLUSION:

• God works in our lives through faith that comes through us receiving His Word through preaching and acting on the faith with endurance for what God has promised us.

21 DAYS OF HEALING
PASTOR JOHN CARMICHAEL
SESSION 4
MESSAGE TITLE: FROM POTENTIAL TO ACTIVATED.

[Act 14:8-10 NASB95] 8 At Lystra a man was sitting who had no strength in his feet, lame from his mother's womb, who had never walked. 9 This man was listening to Paul as he spoke, who, when he had fixed his gaze on him and had seen that he had faith to be made well, 10 said with a loud voice, "Stand upright on your feet." And he leaped up and [began] to walk.

INTRODUCTION:

- Randy Clark recently said we could have "an expectation that you can do it (sic: live in the power of God) as a heaven-and-earth person, bringing God's power to bear every day." FB 06/08/2021
- FB Notes: God intended His message to be accompanied by miraculous signs confirming His Word's truth and power.
- It does not always convince, but it does confirm. (Funny story about Greek god legend: Zeus Hermes – beggars – 2 kind people – everyone else killed.)
- We are called to preach the Gospel of Jesus and release the power of the Holy Spirit.
- While there is more to experience than we are currently experiencing, we can grow.
- In Acts 14, Paul and Barnabas are used to bring healing to a man.

  O V. 8 – insignificant city (Lystra) destitute condition (lame, birth, never walked)

  O V. 9 – Man hears the Word of the Gospel.

O V. 9 – His faith was observed by Paul (through the Holy Spirit?)

O V. 9-10 – His faith was potential and needed to be activated.

O V. 10 – He was healed (jumped up, walked).

Interrogative: What can we learn about God and experience His miracles in our lives from Act 14:8-10?

Transitional: Here are five things we can learn about God and how to experience His miracles in our lives from Acts 14:8-10.

BODY:

I.   God is interested in fixing insignificant and destitute situations.

A.   8 At Lystra a man was sitting who had no strength in his feet, lame from his mother's womb, who had never walked.

B.   No name, but it mattered greatly.

II. God wants us to preach and hear the Gospel.

A.   This man was listening to Paul as he spoke.

B.   LITS Commentary: likely to include some teaching on the healing ministry of Jesus and the power of the Holy Spirit.

C.   [Act 14:7 NASB95] 7 and there they continued to preach the gospel.

D.   [ACT 14:3 NASB95] 3 THEREFORE THEY SPENT A LONG TIME [THERE] SPEAKING BOLDLY [WITH RELIANCE] UPON THE LORD, WHO WAS TESTIFYING TO THE WORD OF HIS GRACE, GRANTING THAT SIGNS AND WONDERS BE DONE BY THEIR HANDS.

E.   APPROACHES TO THE THEOLOGY OF THE GOSPEL:

1. 1. Recreated.

2. Victory over sin, Satan.

3. Price paid.

4. Example – a healed healer.

III. God, at minimum, meets us at our faith level.

A.   9 WHO, WHEN HE HAD FIXED HIS GAZE ON HIM AND HAD SEEN THAT HE HAD FAITH TO BE MADE WELL.

B.   HOW DID PAUL KNOW? HOLY SPIRIT?

C.   HERE, THE MAN HAD FAITH TO BE HEALED.

IV. God wants our potential faith to be activated.

A.   9 THIS MAN WAS LISTENING TO PAUL AS HE SPOKE, WHO, WHEN HE HAD FIXED HIS GAZE ON HIM AND HAD SEEN THAT HE HAD FAITH TO BE MADE WELL, 10 SAID WITH A LOUD VOICE, "STAND UPRIGHT ON YOUR FEET."

B.   [ACT 9:34, 40 NASB95] 34 PETER SAID TO HIM, "AENEAS, JESUS CHRIST HEALS YOU; GET UP AND MAKE YOUR BED." IMMEDIATELY HE GOT UP. ... 40 BUT PETER SENT THEM ALL OUT AND KNELT DOWN AND PRAYED, AND TURNING TO THE BODY, HE SAID, "TABITHA, ARISE." AND SHE OPENED HER EYES, AND WHEN SHE SAW PETER, SHE SAT UP.

V.   God can turn any situation around.

A.   10 AND HE LEAPED UP AND [BEGAN] TO WALK.

B.   FULL MIRACLE FOR FULL FAITH.

C.   GOD WILL WORK IN YOUR LIFE, TOO!

CONCLUSION:

• No matter how insignificant or destitute our situation is, when we allow faith to be built by hearing the Word of God and activate that faith, God will turn that situation around.

• Never give up on your situation. Declare and receive God's Word in your situation. Be honest with your faith level. Act on your faith.

21 DAYS OF HEALING
PASTOR JOHN CARMICHAEL
SESSION 5
MESSAGE TITLE: UNUSUAL MIRACLES.

[Act 19:11-12 NASB95] 11 God was performing extraordinary miracles by the hands of Paul, 12 so that handkerchiefs or aprons were even carried from his body to the sick, and the diseases left them and the evil spirits went out.

INTRODUCTION:

- We are living in unusual times. Things (good and bad) are happening that have never happened before.
- Acts 19:11 tells of unusual things God was doing.
- Text:
  - O God did it.
  - O Unusual and impossible things.
  - O Through the hands of Paul.
- I believe God wants to know that just as we are experiencing unusual negative things, He wants to do unusual, powerful things in our lives today.

Interrogative: How does this affect our faith today?

Transitional: There are three aspects of this passage that affect our faith today.

BODY:

I. God is still doing great things today.

A. [HEB 13:8 NASB95] 8 JESUS CHRIST [IS] THE SAME YESTERDAY AND TODAY AND FOREVER.

B.   THERE IS NO DAY OF MIRACLES. GOD IS A GOD OF MIRACLES.

C.   BELIEVE THAT GOD IS GOING TO DO GREAT THINGS TODAY.

II. There is nothing too hard for God today.

A.   [GEN 18:9-15 NASB95] 9 THEN THEY SAID TO HIM, "WHERE IS SARAH YOUR WIFE?" AND HE SAID, "THERE, IN THE TENT." 10 HE SAID, "I WILL SURELY RETURN TO YOU AT THIS TIME NEXT YEAR; AND BEHOLD, SARAH YOUR WIFE WILL HAVE A SON." AND SARAH WAS LISTENING AT THE TENT DOOR, WHICH WAS BEHIND HIM. 11 NOW ABRAHAM AND SARAH WERE OLD, ADVANCED IN AGE; SARAH WAS PAST CHILDBEARING. 12 SARAH LAUGHED TO HERSELF, SAYING, "AFTER I HAVE BECOME OLD, SHALL I HAVE PLEASURE, MY LORD BEING OLD ALSO?" 13 AND THE LORD SAID TO ABRAHAM, "WHY DID SARAH LAUGH, SAYING, 'SHALL I INDEED BEAR [A CHILD,] WHEN I AM [SO] OLD?' 14 "IS ANYTHING TOO DIFFICULT FOR THE LORD? AT THE APPOINTED TIME I WILL RETURN TO YOU, AT THIS TIME NEXT YEAR, AND SARAH WILL HAVE A SON." 15 SARAH DENIED [IT] HOWEVER, SAYING, "I DID NOT LAUGH"; FOR SHE WAS AFRAID. AND HE SAID, "NO, BUT YOU DID LAUGH."

B.   THE EXTRAORDINARY MIRACLES FROM GOD THROUGH PAUL WERE THINGS THAT HAD NEVER HAPPENED BEFORE, BUT THERE WERE HAPPENING THEN, SOME OF THEM FOR THE FIRST TIME.

C.   BELIEVE IN MIRACLES TODAY—IMPOSSIBLE THINGS.

III. God works through you today.

A. [MAR 9:23 NASB95] 23 AND JESUS SAID TO HIM, " 'IF YOU CAN?' ALL THINGS ARE POSSIBLE TO HIM WHO BELIEVES."

B. MAKE IT PERSONAL.

C. GOD LOVES YOU. HE IS READY TO WORK IN YOUR LIFE.

CONCLUSION
(ATTITUDE OR FEEL, KNOW, DO) (SERMON IN A SENTENCE):

• God wants you to believe in unusual miracles today in your life.

21 DAYS OF HEALING
PASTOR JOHN CARMICHAEL
SESSION 6
MESSAGE TITLE: SPIRITUAL WARFARE OF HEALING.

[Luk 13:10-13 NASB95] 10 And He was teaching in one of the synagogues on the Sabbath. 11 And there was a woman who for eighteen years had had a sickness caused by a spirit; and she was bent double, and could not straighten up at all. 12 When Jesus saw her, He called her over and said to her, "Woman, you are freed from your sickness." 13 And He laid His hands on her; and immediately she was made erect again and [began] glorifying God.

INTRODUCTION:

- There are some who believe that COVID-19 has a demonic component to it. I believe that too.
- Originally, sickness began because of sin and Satan.
- Jesus heals a woman (daughter of Abraham) from a "spirit of infirmity."
- Evidently, sickness has a spiritual warfare aspect that needs to be addressed.

Interrogative: What do we need to know about dealing with the spiritual warfare aspect of receiving divine healing?

Transitional: In Luke 13, we see four things about dealing with the spiritual warfare aspect of receiving divine healing.

BODY
(SCRIPTURE, ILLUSTRATION, ARGUMENTATION, APPLICATION):

I.   The spirit of infirmity is defeated when we receive and release the teaching of the Word of God.

A.   [Luk 13:10 NASB95] 10 And He was teaching in one of the synagogues on the Sabbath.

B.   [Mat 4:23 NASB95] 23 Jesus was going throughout all Galilee, teaching in their synagogues, and proclaiming the gospel of the kingdom, and healing every kind of disease and every kind of sickness among the people.

C.   [Rev 19:15 NASB95] 15 From His mouth comes a sharp sword, so that with it He may strike down the nations, and He will rule them with a rod of iron; and He treads the wine press of the fierce wrath of God, the Almighty.

D.   [Heb 4:12 NASB95] 12 For the word of God is living and active and sharper than any two-edged sword, and piercing as far as the division of soul and spirit, of both joints and marrow, and able to judge the thoughts and intentions of the heart.

II.   The spirit of infirmity attacks people of the covenant too.

A.   [Luk 13:11 NASB95] 11 And there was a woman who for eighteen years had had a sickness caused by a

SPIRIT; AND SHE WAS BENT DOUBLE, AND COULD NOT STRAIGHTEN
UP AT ALL.

B.   [LUK 13:16 NASB95] 16 "AND THIS WOMAN, A
DAUGHTER OF ABRAHAM AS SHE IS, WHOM SATAN HAS BOUND FOR
EIGHTEEN LONG YEARS, SHOULD SHE NOT HAVE BEEN RELEASED
FROM THIS BOND ON THE SABBATH DAY?"

C.   DR. PAUL KING ASKS, "DOES A CHRISTIAN HAVE TO
DEAL WITH SIN AFTER CONVERSION? YES. THEN DOES A CHRISTIAN
HAVE TO DEAL WITH DEMONS AFFECTING THEM AFTER CONVER-
SION? YES. CHRISTIANS CAN BE DEMONIZED BECAUSE THEY CAN BE
INFLUENCED BY, IMPACTED BY, AND TORMENTED BY DEMONS."

D.   DR. RANDY CLARK MENTIONS THAT MANY OF THE
"HEALERS" OF CHRISTIANITY ALSO HAD GREAT DELIVERANCE MIN-
ISTRIES.

E.   SICKNESS OFTEN (ALWAYS?) HAS A SPIRITUAL WARFARE
COMPONENT AND PHYSICAL ISSUES.

F.   [ACT 10:38 NASB95] 38 "[YOU KNOW OF] JESUS OF
NAZARETH, HOW GOD ANOINTED HIM WITH THE HOLY SPIRIT
AND WITH POWER, AND [HOW] HE WENT ABOUT DOING GOOD AND
HEALING ALL WHO WERE OPPRESSED BY THE DEVIL, FOR GOD WAS
WITH HIM.

III. The spirit of infirmity often causes people to think that God is afflicting or neglecting them.

A.   [LUK 13:12 NASB95] 12 WHEN JESUS SAW HER, HE CALLED HER OVER AND SAID TO HER, "WOMAN, YOU ARE FREED FROM YOUR SICKNESS."

B.   THE ENEMY LIES AND BLAMES GOD. IT IS NOT GOD AFFLICTING YOU. IT IS THE ENEMY.

C.   JESUS LOVES YOU. HE DID NOT CAUSE THE PROBLEM, BUT HE WILL FIX IT!

IV. The spirit of infirmity leaves when spoken to, and acts of faith are done.

A.   [LUK 13:13 NASB95] 13 AND HE LAID HIS HANDS ON HER; AND IMMEDIATELY SHE WAS MADE ERECT AGAIN AND [BEGAN] GLORIFYING GOD.

B.   [ACT 28:8-9 NASB95] 8 AND IT HAPPENED THAT THE FATHER OF PUBLIUS WAS LYING [IN BED] AFFLICTED WITH [RECURRENT] FEVER AND DYSENTERY; AND PAUL WENT IN [TO SEE] HIM AND AFTER HE HAD PRAYED, HE LAID HIS HANDS ON HIM AND HEALED HIM. 9 AFTER THIS HAD HAPPENED, THE REST OF THE PEOPLE ON THE ISLAND WHO HAD DISEASES WERE COMING TO HIM AND GETTING CURED.

C.   [JAS 5:14-15 NASB95] 14 IS ANYONE AMONG YOU SICK? [THEN] HE MUST CALL FOR THE ELDERS OF THE CHURCH AND THEY ARE TO PRAY OVER HIM, ANOINTING HIM WITH OIL IN THE NAME OF THE LORD; 15 AND THE PRAYER OFFERED IN FAITH WILL RESTORE THE ONE WHO IS SICK, AND THE LORD WILL RAISE HIM UP, AND IF HE HAS COMMITTED SINS, THEY WILL BE FORGIVEN HIM.

D.   [LUK 4:38-40 NASB95] 38 THEN HE GOT UP AND
[LEFT] THE SYNAGOGUE, AND ENTERED SIMON'S HOME. NOW
SIMON'S MOTHER-IN-LAW WAS SUFFERING FROM A HIGH FEVER, AND
THEY ASKED HIM TO HELP HER. 39 AND STANDING OVER HER, HE
REBUKED THE FEVER, AND IT LEFT HER; AND SHE IMMEDIATELY
GOT UP AND WAITED ON THEM. 40 WHILE THE SUN WAS SETTING,
ALL THOSE WHO HAD ANY [WHO WERE] SICK WITH VARIOUS DISEAS-
ES BROUGHT THEM TO HIM; AND LAYING HIS HANDS ON EACH ONE
OF THEM, HE WAS HEALING THEM.

CONCLUSION:

- We must address the spiritual warfare component to
  receive divine healing.
- Receive and release the Word of God as part of experiencing divine healing.
- Understand that the atonement of Jesus has defeated
  every spirit of infirmity.
- Refuse to believe the lies of the enemy that blame God
  as the cause of sickness.
- Allow yourself to be prayed for, be anointed with oil,
  and have hands laid upon you.

21 DAYS OF HEALING
PASTOR JOHN CARMICHAEL
SESSION 7
MESSAGE TITLE: SIGNIFICANT: YOUR HEALING IS A WORK OF GOD.

[Jhn 9:1-7 NASB95] 1 As He passed by, He saw a man blind from birth. 2 And His disciples asked Him, "Rabbi, who sinned, this man or his parents, that he would be born blind?" 3 Jesus answered, "[It was] neither [that] this man sinned, nor his parents; but [it was] so that the works of God might be displayed in him. 4 " the works of Him who sent Me as long as it is day; night is coming when no one can work. 5 "While I am in the world, I am the Light of the world." 6 When He had said this, He spat on the ground, and made clay of the spittle, and applied the clay to his eyes, 7 and said to him, "Go, wash in the pool of Siloam" (which is translated, Sent). So he went away and washed, and came [back] seeing.

INTRODUCTION:

- This miracle was significant.
- This is one of the "seven sign miracles," according to Stephen Kim.

Interrogative: Why is this healing in John 9 significant to us?

Transitional: The healing in John 9 is significant because it deals with God's doctrine and interaction with us.

BODY:

I. Divine healing deals with a significant doctrine about God.

A. GOD IS NOT THE CAUSE OF SICKNESS.

1. "who sinned"?

2. [Luk 13:1-5 NASB95] 1 Now on the same occasion there were some present who reported to Him about the Galileans whose blood Pilate had mixed with their sacrifices. 2 And Jesus said to them, "Do you suppose that these Galileans were [greater] sinners than all [other] Galileans because they suffered this [fate?] 3 "I tell you, no, but unless you repent, you will all likewise perish. 4 "Or do you suppose that those eighteen on whom the tower in Siloam fell and killed them were [worse] culprits than all the men who live in Jerusalem? 5 "I tell you, no, but unless you repent, you will all likewise perish."

3. SFLB note: the thought was that "individual suffering" was the result of "individual sin."

4. Sin is the cause. Nihimola, "Adam's original sin." Calvin, "sickness was inflicted as a punishment of sin."

5. Schmit: since the results of sin are an open door for sickness, then righteousness provided by Jesus' atonement results in the availability of healing.

6. EC – God did not cause it, but He did cure it.

B.   B. GOD IS WORKING TO ALLEVIATE THE SUFFERING OF
THE SICK.

1. "works of Him"

2. The physical and spiritual healing of the blind man was the work(s) of the Father.

3. [Isa 53:4-5 NASB95] 4 Surely our griefs He Himself bore, And our sorrows He carried; Yet we ourselves esteemed Him stricken, Smitten of God, and afflicted. 5 But He was pierced through for our transgressions, He was crushed for our iniquities; The chastening for our well-being [fell] upon Him, And by His scourging we are healed.

4. [Mat 8:16-17 NASB95] 16 When evening came, they brought to Him many who were demon-possessed; and He cast out the spirits with a word, and healed all who were ill. 17 [This was] to fulfill what was spoken through Isaiah the prophet: "HE HIMSELF TOOK OUR INFIRMITIES AND CARRIED AWAY OUR DISEASES."

5. God does not deal only one part of us. It is a false Platonic idea (inner person is good while the outer person is bad.)

C.   GOD HAS COMMISSIONED US TO HELP HUMANITY.

1. "We must work."

2. NKJV – "I must work…" NASB – "We must work…"

3. Significant in understanding the mission of healing.

4. Howard Ervin – prayer and anointing with oil is an ongoing ministry of the Church. "Command" and "promise" of healing in Mark 16.

5. The blind man was commanded to go to the pool of Siloam (sent).

6. Jesus was sent to the blind man. Then the blind man was sent.

II. Divine healing demonstrates God's significant interaction with us.

A.   GOD IS CONCERNED AND ACTIVE IN OUR BODY.

1. [Psa 139:13 NASB95] 13 For You formed my inward parts; You wove me in my mother's womb.

2. [1Th 5:23 NASB95] 23 Now may the God of peace Himself sanctify you entirely; and may your spirit and soul and body be preserved complete, without blame at the coming of our Lord Jesus Christ.

3. [Gen 2:7 NASB95] 7 Then the LORD God formed man of dust from the ground, and breathed into his nostrils the breath of life; and man became a living being.

B.   GOD WANTS TO RECREATE US ACCORDING TO HIS ORIGINAL PLAN.

1. Picture of creation. Some commentators believe that Jesus packed the eye socket with mud or created an eyeball with the mud.

2. Irenaeus – picture of recreation of man.

3. He wants to restore us to His original plan for us.

4. Jesus healed by the Holy Spirit (Acts 10:38) Who was present at Creation (Gen 1:2).

C.   GOD USES MANY METHODS TO HEAL US AND THROUGH US.

1. Gen 2:7 – ground (natural) and breath (divine)

2. Millard – medicine and faith produce healing.

3. Oral Roberts praying hands is a picture of the interaction of medicine and faith.

CONCLUSION
(ATTITUDE OR FEEL, KNOW, DO) (SERMON IN A SENTENCE):

• The healing of your body is significant to God and His mission.
  O Work by faith (pray, confession, meditate, seek all roads of healing) for your healing as His Will for you because of the atonement Jesus provided.
  O Make it a point to preach and pray for the healing of others in this world as being commissioned by God.

21 DAYS OF HEALING
PASTOR JOHN CARMICHAEL
SESSION 8
MESSAGE TITLE:
LIFE FROM THE DEAD: GOD'S WAYS GOD'S MIRACLES.

[2Ki 13:21 NASB] 21 As they were burying a man, behold, they saw a marauding band; and they cast the man into the grave of Elisha. And when the man touched the bones of Elisha he revived and stood up on his feet.

INTRODUCTION:

- God's ways confuse people. This becomes a challenge to people's faith.

Interrogative: What can we learn from the Elisha bone resurrection?

Transitional: We can learn from a couple of principles from the story's people.

BODY:

I. The People

A.   ELISHA

1. [2Ki 2:9 NASB] 9 When they had crossed over, Elijah said to Elisha, "Ask what I shall do for you before I am taken from you." And Elisha said, "Please, let a double portion of your spirit be upon me."

2. One miracle left for the double portion. Then died. God fulfilled.

3. [1Th 5:24 NASB] 24 Faithful is He who calls you, and He also will bring it to pass.

4. God will always fulfill His promise.

B. THE DEAD MAN

1. [2Ki 13:21 NASB] 21 As they were burying a man, behold, they saw a marauding band; and they cast the man into the grave of Elisha. And when the man touched the bones of Elisha he revived and stood up on his feet.

2. It is NOT OVER!

3. He is on his feet. Not partial resurrections!

4. God is not done with you!

C. OTHERS

1. [1Ki 18:44 NASB] 44 It came about at the seventh [time,] that he said, "Behold, a cloud as small as a man's hand is coming up from the sea." And he said, "Go up, say to Ahab, 'Prepare [your chariot] and go down, so that the [heavy] shower does not stop you.'"

2. They were one man down (the one who died). But God resurrected him.

3. God said, "Look again!"

II. The Principles

A.   GOD'S WAYS MUST BE TRUSTED.

1. Timing? Delay? Don't be so quick to blame God for those.

2. [Jhn 15:7 NASB] 7 "If you abide in Me, and My words abide in you, ask whatever you wish, and it will be done for you.

3. Trust Him to do His part. No assumptions.

B.   GOD'S MIRACLES MUST BE BELIEVED.

1. Many times, God does things that we believe Him for.

2. Rom 4:17 NASB] 17 (as it is written, "A FATHER OF MANY NATIONS HAVE I MADE YOU") in the presence of Him whom he believed, [even] God, who gives life to the dead and calls into being that which does not exist.

CONCLUSION:

- God fulfills His promises as we trust Him and believe in Him.

21 DAYS OF HEALING
PASTOR JOHN CARMICHAEL
SESSION 9
MESSAGE TITLE: SERPENT ON A POLE.

[Num 21:4-9 NASB] 4 Then they set out from Mount Hor by the way of the Red Sea, to go around the land of Edom; and the people became impatient because of the journey. 5 The people spoke against God and Moses, "Why have you brought us up out of Egypt to die in the wilderness? For there is no food and no water, and we loathe this miserable food." 6 The LORD sent fiery serpents among the people and they bit the people, so that many people of Israel died. 7 So the people came to Moses and said, "We have sinned, because we have spoken against the LORD and you; intercede with the LORD, that He may remove the serpents from us." And Moses interceded for the people. 8 Then the LORD said to Moses, "Make a fiery [serpent,] and set it on a standard; and it shall come about, that everyone who is bitten, when he looks at it, he will live." 9 And Moses made a bronze serpent and set it on the standard; and it came about, that if a serpent bit any man, when he looked to the bronze serpent, he lived.

INTRODUCTION:

- The medical symbol has some confusion as to its meaning. First, there are two symbols. One has a pole and one snack. The other has one pole with wings and two snakes. Secondly, there is disagreement as to the origin. According to the website Early Church History, the origin of the symbol is the story of Moses and the fiery serpent on a pole. (https://earlychurchhistory.org/medicine/the-biblical-caduceus-symbol-of-medicine/)
- Just like there is confusion about the medical symbol. The camp of Israel was confused about how healing

would come. There is confusion as to God being a Healer.

- The confusion caused poor theology and practice then. It causes poor theology and practice now.

Interrogative: What can this story tell us about healing?

Transitional: There are three truths we can learn about healing from this passage.

BODY:

I.   Sin is a cause of sickness.

A.   THEIR GRUMBLING WAS TWO THINGS.

1. It was doubt.

2. It was disobedience.

B.   NOT EVERYONE GRUMBLED, BUT ALL HAD TO DEAL WITH IT.

C.   ORIGINAL SIN IN THE GARDEN IS THE SOURCE OF SICKNESS. IT WAS ON THE DAY THE FIRST COUPLE EAT OF THE FORBIDDEN FRUIT THAT DEATH AND DISEASE CAME. GENESIS 2:17.

II.   Don't worship the method, only the Source of healing.

A.   NEHUSHTAN

B.   [2KI 18:4 NASB] 4 HE REMOVED THE HIGH PLACES AND BROKE DOWN THE [SACRED] PILLARS AND CUT DOWN THE

ASHERAH. HE ALSO BROKE IN PIECES THE BRONZE SERPENT THAT MOSES HAD MADE, FOR UNTIL THOSE DAYS THE SONS OF ISRAEL BURNED INCENSE TO IT; AND IT WAS CALLED NEHUSHTAN.

III. God is the source of healing.

A.   IT SEEMS OBVIOUS THAT GOD WANTED TO BE THE SOURCE OF THE HEALING.

B.   HE PROVIDED A PATH TO HEALING.

C.   EXODUS 15:26 TELLS US THAT THE NATURE OF GOD IS TO HEAL.

CONCLUSION:

- The pericope of the serpent on the pole demonstrates the source of sickness is the failure of humans, but that God desires to be the source of all healing and that we should not worship a methodology.

21 DAYS OF HEALING
PASTOR JOHN CARMICHAEL
SESSION 10
MESSAGE TITLE: THIS IS SICK! JESUS IS THE HEALER, AND THAT
IS WHY IT MATTERS.

[Isa 53:4-5 NASB] 4 Surely our griefs He Himself bore, And our sorrows He carried; Yet we ourselves esteemed Him stricken, Smitten of God, and afflicted. 5 But He was pierced through for our transgressions, He was crushed for our iniquities; The chastening for our well-being [fell] upon Him, And by His scourging we are healed.

[Act 10:38 NASB] 38 "[You know of] Jesus of Nazareth, how God anointed Him with the Holy Spirit and with power, and [how] He went about doing good and healing all who were oppressed by the devil, for God was with Him.

[1Co 2:3-6 NASB] 3 I was with you in weakness and in fear and in much trembling, 4 and my message and my preaching were not in persuasive words of wisdom, but in demonstration of the Spirit and of power, 5 so that your faith would not rest on the wisdom of men, but on the power of God. 6 Yet we do speak wisdom among those who are mature; a wisdom, however, not of this age nor of the rulers of this age, who are passing away; . . .

INTRODUCTION:

- This world is sick. We are sick in several ways.
- Spiritually sick. Antichrist/cold/lukewarm, sin, curse, demonic
- Emotionally/Relationally sick. Oppressed/fearful/ depressed. Angry/divided/strife.
- Physically sick. COVID-19. Many other diseases.

- Sickness resulted from the fall in the Garden of Eden. Healing came as a result of Jesus' atonement.

Interrogative (attitude or feel, know, do): What does believing in and demonstrating divine healing reveals about God, and why does it matter today?

Transitional: Believing in and demonstrating divine healing reveals three things about God to this world.

BODY:

I.   Three points of the texts

A.   DIVINE HEALING IS A DEMONSTRATION OF GOD'S LOVE.

B.   DIVINE HEALING COMES FROM GOD'S POWER.

C.   DIVINE HEALING IS GOOD.

II. Three points of application

A.   LET'S SHOW THE WORLD GOD CARES ABOUT THEM.

1. The substitutionary, sacrificial death, burial, and resurrection of Jesus Christ shows God's love.

2. [Rom 5:8 NASB] 8 But God demonstrates His own love toward us, in that while we were yet sinners, Christ died for us.

B.   LET'S SHOW THE WORLD THAT GOD IS POWERFUL.

1. Divine healing is easy for God but hard for man.

2. [Mar 16:19-20 NASB] 19 So then, when the Lord Jesus had spoken to them, He was received up into heaven and sat down at the right hand of God. 20 And they went out and preached everywhere, while the Lord worked with them, and confirmed the word by the signs that followed.] [[And they promptly reported all these instructions to Peter and his companions. And after that, Jesus Himself sent out through them from east to west the sacred and imperishable proclamation of eternal salvation.]]

C.   LET'S SHOW THE WORLD THAT GOD IS GOOD.

1. Jesus' healing and deliverance ministry was good.

2. God is good. This was one of the pillars of Oral Roberts' healing ministry.

3. Sickness is bad. Healing is good.

CONCLUSION:

- Believe in and preach God's love.
- Believe in and preach God's power.
- Believe in and preach God's goodness.

21 DAYS OF HEALING
PASTOR JOHN CARMICHAEL
SESSION 11
MESSAGE TITLE: RISING UP FROM WHAT HAS YOU BEND DOWN
DEFEATING THE SPIRIT OF INFIRMITY.

[Luk 13:10-17 NASB] 10 And He was teaching in one of the synagogues on the Sabbath. 11 And there was a woman who for eighteen years had had a sickness caused by a spirit; and she was bent double, and could not straighten up at all. 12 When Jesus saw her, He called her over and said to her, "Woman, you are freed from your sickness." 13 And He laid His hands on her; and immediately she was made erect again and [began] glorifying God. 14 But the synagogue official, indignant because Jesus had healed on the Sabbath, [began] saying to the crowd in response, "There are six days in which work should be done; so come during them and get healed, and not on the Sabbath day." 15 But the Lord answered him and said, "You hypocrites, does not each of you on the Sabbath untie his ox or his donkey from the stall and lead him away to water [him?] 16 "And this woman, a daughter of Abraham as she is, whom Satan has bound for eighteen long years, should she not have been released from this bond on the Sabbath day?" 17 As He said this, all His opponents were being humiliated; and the entire crowd was rejoicing over all the glorious things being done by Him.

INTRODUCTION:

- A demon spirit can cause physical sickness. Spirits affect the physical world. Many ailments are caused by living in the fallen world. Many healings make no mention of demons. Yet, spirits can and do attack our bodies, emotions, and thinking patterns.

Interrogative: What can this text teach us about getting free from spirits that impact infirmity?

Transitional: Here are seven important lessons about getting free from spirits that impact infirmity.

BODY:

I. The Text:

A.   RIGHT ENVIRONMENT V 10

B.   WRONG CONDITION V 11

C.   JESUS RESPONDS V 12-13

D.   ENEMY RESPONDS V 14

E.   JESUS CORRECTS V 15

F.   IDENTITY ESTABLISHED V 16

G.   HE/WE WIN V17

II. The Sermon:

F.   GET IN THE RIGHT ENVIRONMENT.

1. [Psa 92:13 NASB] 13 Planted in the house of the LORD, They will flourish in the courts of our God.

2. She got in the right environment to be free.

3. The environment can influence our freedom. Being in a community with a church where they worship and the Word of God is preached can influence our freedom.

G.   UNDERSTAND YOUR CONDITION.

1.   [2Co 2:11 NASB] 11 so that no advantage would be taken of us by Satan, for we are not ignorant of his schemes.

2.   We must realize we are in a cosmic battle against a deadly foe. This enemy affects us in many ways, including our physical health.

H.   ALLOW GOD TO WORK.

1.   1. [Phl 2:12-13 NASB] 12 So then, my beloved, just as you have always obeyed, not as in my presence only, but now much more in my absence, work out your salvation with fear and trembling; 13 for it is God who is at work in you, both to will and to work for [His] good pleasure.

2.   2. He sees, calls, proclaims faith, and releases the power.

I.   PREPARE FOR RETALIATION.

1.   [1Pe 4:12-13 NASB] 12 Beloved, do not be surprised at the fiery ordeal among you, which comes upon you for your testing, as though some strange thing were happening to you; 13 but to the degree that you share the sufferings of Christ, keep on rejoicing, so that also at the revelation of His glory you may rejoice with exultation.

2.   Not everyone will support what God is doing in your life. Some will not understand and therefore respond inappropriately.

J.   GET THE RIGHT PRIORITIES.

1. [Mat 6:33 NASB] 33 "But seek first His kingdom and His righteousness, and all these things will be added to you.

2. We must be willing to put aside our own thoughts and opinions to see God's thoughts and opinions. We must allow God's ways to upend our theology and practice. We are seeking His Ways and operating in His Kingdom.

K.   BE RENEWED IN YOUR IDENTITY.

1. [Rom 12:2 NASB] 2 And do not be conformed to this world, but be transformed by the renewing of your mind, so that you may prove what the will of God is, that which is good and acceptable and perfect.

2. The more we know that we are children of God and have divinely granted spiritual authority, the more we can have the confidence to walk in victory over the enemy of our lives.

L.   EXPECT JESUS AND YOU TO WIN.

1. [2Co 2:14 NASB] 14 But thanks be to God, who always leads us in triumph in Christ, and manifests through us the sweet aroma of the knowledge of Him in every place.

2. God's wisdom and power will free you from deception, allowing freedom from the demonic.

CONCLUSION:

- Jesus wants you free from every demonic spirit that influences infirmity.

21 DAYS OF HEALING
PASTOR JOHN CARMICHAEL
SESSION 12
MESSAGE TITLE: MINISTRY JESUS STYLE

[Act 10:38 NASB] 38 "[You know of] Jesus of Nazareth, how God anointed Him with the Holy Spirit and with power, and [how] He went about doing good and healing all who were oppressed by the devil, for God was with Him.

INTRODUCTION:

- Nazareth—Jesus' earthly ministry was accomplished because God anointed Him with the Holy Spirit
- He serves as an example of how the church will minister today.

Interrogative: What can we learn from this passage that can direct us in ministry?

Transitional: There are three aspects of Jesus' earthly ministry that we can learn from Acts 10:38 for ministry today.

BODY:

I.   God is our empowerment.

A. ". . . how God anointed Him with the Holy Spirit and with power . . ."

B. [Luk 4:18-19 NASB] 18 "THE SPIRIT OF THE LORD IS UPON ME, BECAUSE HE ANOINTED ME TO PREACH THE GOSPEL

TO THE POOR. HE HAS SENT ME TO PROCLAIM RELEASE TO THE CAPTIVES, AND RECOVERY OF SIGHT TO THE BLIND, TO SET FREE THOSE WHO ARE OPPRESSED, 19 TO PROCLAIM THE FAVORABLE YEAR OF THE LORD."

C. [1Sa 16:12-13 NASB] 12 So he sent and brought him in. Now he was ruddy, with beautiful eyes and a handsome appearance. And the LORD said, "Arise, anoint him; for this is he." 13 Then Samuel took the horn of oil and anointed him in the midst of his brothers; and the Spirit of the LORD came mightily upon David from that day forward. And Samuel arose and went to Ramah.

D. This is seen at the new birth. [2Co 1:21-22 NASB] 21 Now He who establishes us with you in Christ and anointed us is God, 22 who also sealed us and gave [us] the Spirit in our hearts as a pledge.

E. This is after the new birth. [Act 1:5, 8 NASB] 5 for John baptized with water, but you will be baptized with the Holy Spirit not many days from now." ... 8 but you will receive power when the Holy Spirit has come upon you; and you shall be My witnesses both in Jerusalem, and in all Judea and Samaria, and even to the remotest part of the earth."

F. Notice that Jesus went in "full of the Holy Spirit" (Lk 4:1), and came out "in the power of the Holy Spirit" (Lk 4:14). This could be a picture of the believer. We receive the Holy Spirit in us at the new birth. We walk in the power of the Holy Spirit after the baptism in the Holy Spirit.

G. [Act 2:1 NASB] 1 When the day of Pentecost had come, they were all together in one place.

H. What do we see in David's anointing, Jesus' anointing, and the Pentecostal anointing? Three aspects:

1. 1.Submission to God.

2. 2.Seeking God.

3. 3.Separated unto God.

J. God never expects us to accomplish ministry without Him. As we submit, seek, and separate ourselves unto Him, we will walk in the empowerment portion of the anointing of the Holy Spirit.

II. God challenges us to engage.

A. ". . . [how] He went about doing good and healing all who were oppressed by the devil . . ."

B. Oppressed: to exercise harsh control.

C. [Act 1:5, 8 NASB] 5 for John baptized with water, but you will be baptized with the Holy Spirit not many days from now." ... 8 but you will receive power when the Holy Spirit has come upon you; and you shall be My witnesses both in Jerusalem, and in all Judea and Samaria, and even to the remotest part of the earth."

D.[Mar 16:15-18 NASB] 15 And He said to them, "Go into all the world and preach the gospel to all creation. 16 "He who has believed and has been baptized shall be saved; but he who has disbelieved shall be condemned. 17 "These signs will accompany those who have believed: in My name they will cast out demons, they will speak with new tongues;

18 they will pick up serpents, and if they drink any deadly [poison,] it will not hurt them; they will lay hands on the sick, and they will recover."

E.[Eph 6:12 NASB] 12 For our struggle is not against flesh and blood, but against the rulers, against the powers, against the world forces of this darkness, against the spiritual [forces] of wickedness in the heavenly [places.]

F.[Mar 3:27 NASB] 27 "But no one can enter the strong man's house and plunder his property unless he first binds the strong man, and then he will plunder his house.

G.[Luk 10:17 NASB] 17 The seventy returned with joy, saying, "Lord, even the demons are subject to us in Your name."

III. God is our encouragement.

A. ". . . for God was with Him."

B. [Rom 8:31 NASB] 31 What then shall we say to these things? If God [is] for us, who [is] against us?

CONCLUSION:

- Expect the empowerment of the Holy Spirit as you submit, seek, and separate yourself unto God.
- Engage in the mission of evangelism. Share your faith. Believe for healing. Take authority over the devil.
- • Be encouraged. God is with you.

21 DAYS OF HEALING
PASTOR JOHN CARMICHAEL
SESSION 13
MESSAGE TITLE: MADE FOR MIRACLES

Romans 15:18 For I will not dare to speak of anything except what Christ has accomplished through me, to make the Gentiles obedient, by word and deed, 19 by the power of signs and wonders, by the power of the Spirit of God, so that from Jerusalem and as far around as Illyricum, I have fully preached the gospel of Christ. (MEV)

INTRODUCTION:

- If you do not understand the purpose of a thing, abuse is inevitable.
- Miracles are often misunderstood. This causes neglect or abuse.
- The church is made for miracles. It has always been part of Christianity.
- Martin Luther - "If the Christian has the faith, he shall have power to do these signs. ...For a Christian has equal power with Christ, is one cake with him. ...Where there is a Christian, there is therefore the power to do such signs even now if it is necessary."
- John Wesley – "Wesley believed that the supernatural almost disappeared in Christendom, but not because God had withdrawn the gifts. "From this time (Constantinian era) they (gifts) almost totally ceased; ...The real cause was, 'the love of many,' almost of all Christians, so called, was 'waxed cold.' The Christians had no more of the Spirit of Christ than the other Heathens. ...the

Christians were turned Heathens again, and had only a
dead form left."
- Wesley - "I do not recollect any scripture wherein we are
taught that miracles were to be confined within limits
either of the apostolic or the Cyprianic age; or of any
period of time, longer or shorter, even till the restitution
of all things."
- The Apostle Paul gives us 6 aspects of what it means to
be Made for Miracles.

Interrogative: What does it mean to be "made for miracles?"

Transitional: Here are seven aspects of what it means to be "made
for miracles."

I.   Made for miracles means we are Christ-Centered.

A.   V. 17-18 - 17 IN CHRIST JESUS THEREFORE I HAVE REA-
SON TO BOAST IN MY SERVICE TO GOD. 18 FOR I WILL NOT DARE
TO SPEAK OF ANYTHING EXCEPT WHAT CHRIST HAS ACCOMPLISHED
THROUGH ME

B.   CHRIST GETS THE GLORY. CHRIST IS THE MESSAGE.
CHRIST IS THE FOCUS.

C.   I CORINTHIANS 2:1-2 - BROTHERS, WHEN I CAME TO
YOU, I DID NOT COME WITH SUPERIORITY OF SPEECH OR WISDOM,
DECLARING TO YOU THE TESTIMONY OF GOD. 2 FOR I DETER-
MINED NOT TO KNOW ANYTHING AMONG YOU EXCEPT JESUS
CHRIST AND HIM CRUCIFIED.

D.   MIRACLES ARE A RESULT OF THE REDEMPTIVE WORK OF
JESUS CHRIST.

E.   WHEN WE BELIEVE FOR MIRACLES, WE ARE ACTING LIKE JESUS CHRIST.

II.   Made for miracles means we are Spirit-empowered

A.   V. 15-16 - 15 NEVERTHELESS, BROTHERS, I HAVE WRITTEN EVEN MORE BOLDLY TO YOU ON SOME POINTS, TO REMIND YOU, BECAUSE OF THE GRACE THAT IS GIVEN TO ME FROM GOD, 16 THAT I MIGHT BE A MINISTER OF JESUS CHRIST TO THE GENTILES, IN THE PRIESTLY SERVICE OF THE GOSPEL OF GOD, SO THAT THE OFFERING OF THE GENTILES MIGHT BE ACCEPTABLE, BEING SANCTIFIED BY THE HOLY SPIRIT.

B.   V. 18-19 - 18 FOR I WILL NOT DARE TO SPEAK OF ANYTHING EXCEPT WHAT CHRIST HAS ACCOMPLISHED THROUGH ME, TO MAKE THE GENTILES OBEDIENT, BY WORD AND DEED, 19 BY THE POWER OF SIGNS AND WONDERS, BY THE POWER OF THE SPIRIT OF GOD, SO THAT FROM JERUSALEM AND AS FAR AROUND AS ILLYRICUM, I HAVE FULLY PREACHED THE GOSPEL OF CHRIST.

C.   MIRACLES ARE NOT HUMAN ACCOMPLISHMENTS.

D.   "IN THE POWER" OR "BY THE POWER"

E.   DR. THIMELL - THE DAY OF PENTECOST WAS NOT THE CHURCH'S BIRTHDAY. RATHER, THE DAY OF PENTECOST WAS THE BEGINNING OF THE CHURCH'S EMPOWERMENT. THE CHURCH HAD ALREADY BEEN BIRTHED WHEN JESUS BREATHED ON THE DISCIPLES AFTER HIS RESURRECTION AND SAID, "RECEIVE YE THE HOLY SPIRIT." (JN. 20:22) THE NEW COVENANT WAS INITIATED ALREADY PRIOR TO THE DAY OF PENTECOST. ALL THAT REMAINED WAS THEIR NEED FOR EMPOWERMENT, FOR THEIR COMMISSION WAS AN IMPOS-

SIBLE ONE WITHOUT SUPERNATURAL ENABLEMENT. JESUS FULFILLED THE OLD COVENANT AND ESTABLISHED A NEW ONE, SEALED BY THE SHEDDING OF HIS OWN BLOOD. THEN, AS THE RESURRECTED, ASCENDED LORD, HE EMPOWERED THE MEMBERS OF HIS CHURCH WITH SPIRIT BAPTISM, EQUIPPING THEM FOR THEIR MISSION TO TAKE THE GOSPEL TO THE UTTERMOST PARTS OF THE EARTH.

F.   MIRACLES ARE NOT FROM OR FOCUSED ON HUMANITY, BUT FROM AND FOCUSED ON HIM!

G.   SEEK NOT TO GLORIFY THOSE USED IN MIRACLES NOR SEEK GLORY FOR YOURSELF. GIVE HIM THE GLORY!

H.   YIELD YOURSELF TO THE HOLY SPIRIT AND WATCH HIM PERFORM MIRACLES.

III. Made for miracles means we are Word confirming.

A.   V. 18-19 - 18 FOR I WILL NOT DARE TO SPEAK OF ANYTHING EXCEPT WHAT CHRIST HAS ACCOMPLISHED THROUGH ME, TO MAKE THE GENTILES OBEDIENT, BY WORD AND DEED, 19 BY THE POWER OF SIGNS AND WONDERS, BY THE POWER OF THE SPIRIT OF GOD, SO THAT FROM JERUSALEM AND AS FAR AROUND AS ILLYRICUM, I HAVE FULLY PREACHED THE GOSPEL OF CHRIST.

B.   MORRIS – PAUL CONSIDERED "BARE" PREACHING WITHOUT THE ACTIVE AND SOMETIMES MIRACULOUS WORK OF THE HOLY SPIRIT EVIDENT TO BE LESS THAN FULLY PREACHING THE GOSPEL.

C.   I THESSALONIANS 1:5 (MEV) - FOR OUR GOSPEL DID NOT COME TO YOU IN WORD ONLY, BUT ALSO IN POWER, AND IN

THE HOLY SPIRIT, AND IN MUCH ASSURANCE, JUST AS YOU KNOW WHAT KIND OF MEN WE WERE AMONG YOU FOR YOUR SAKE.

D.   I CORINTHIANS 2:3-5 I WAS WITH YOU IN WEAKNESS AND IN FEAR AND IN MUCH TREMBLING, 4 AND MY MESSAGE AND MY PREACHING WERE NOT IN PERSUASIVE WORDS OF WISDOM, BUT IN DEMONSTRATION OF THE SPIRIT AND OF POWER, 5 SO THAT YOUR FAITH WOULD NOT [C]REST ON THE WISDOM OF MEN, BUT ON THE POWER OF GOD.

E.   MARK 16:19 - 19 AFTER THE LORD HAD SPOKEN TO THEM, HE WAS RECEIVED UP INTO HEAVEN AND SAT AT THE RIGHT HAND OF GOD. 20 THEN THEY WENT FORTH AND PREACHED EVERYWHERE, THE LORD WORKING WITH THEM AND CONFIRMING THE WORD THROUGH THE ACCOMPANYING SIGNS. AMEN.

F.   MIRACLES ARE NOT A SUBSTITUTE FOR THE WORD. THEY SUPPLEMENT THE WORD.

G.   PRIORITIZE THE PREACHED WORD TO SEE MIRACLES.

IV. Made for miracles means we are divinely mandated.

A.   V. 18-19 - 18 FOR I WILL NOT DARE TO SPEAK OF ANY-THING EXCEPT WHAT CHRIST HAS ACCOMPLISHED THROUGH ME, TO MAKE THE GENTILES OBEDIENT, BY WORD AND DEED, 19 BY THE POWER OF SIGNS AND WONDERS, BY THE POWER OF THE SPIRIT OF GOD, SO THAT FROM JERUSALEM AND AS FAR AROUND AS ILLYRI-CUM, I HAVE FULLY PREACHED THE GOSPEL OF CHRIST.

B.   MIRACLE MINISTRY MUST BE SEEN AS COMMISSIONED BY THE LORD JESUS CHRIST.

C.   MARK 16:15 HE SAID TO THEM, "GO INTO ALL THE WORLD, AND PREACH THE GOSPEL TO EVERY CREATURE. 16 HE WHO BELIEVES AND IS BAPTIZED WILL BE SAVED. BUT HE WHO DOES NOT BELIEVE WILL BE CONDEMNED. 17 THESE SIGNS WILL ACCOMPANY THOSE WHO BELIEVE: IN MY NAME THEY WILL CAST OUT DEMONS; THEY WILL SPEAK WITH NEW TONGUES; 18 THEY WILL TAKE UP SERPENTS; IF THEY DRINK ANY DEADLY THING, IT WILL NOT HURT THEM; THEY WILL LAY HANDS ON THE SICK, AND THEY WILL RECOVER."

D.   CHRISTIANITY IS MADE FOR MIRACLES. BELIEVE FOR MIRACLES.

V.   Made for miracles means we are outwardly focused.

A.   V. 19 - 19 BY THE POWER OF SIGNS AND WONDERS, BY THE POWER OF THE SPIRIT OF GOD, SO THAT FROM JERUSALEM AND AS FAR AROUND AS ILLYRICUM, I HAVE FULLY PREACHED THE GOSPEL OF CHRIST.

B.   "ILLYRICUM" EXTREME NORTH-WESTERN GREECE.

C.   STARTING HOME (FROM JERUSALEM) TO THE EXTREME (ILLYRICUM).

D.   ACTS 1:8 BUT YOU WILL RECEIVE POWER WHEN THE HOLY SPIRIT HAS COME UPON YOU; AND YOU SHALL BE MY WITNESSES BOTH IN JERUSALEM, AND IN ALL JUDEA AND SAMARIA, AND EVEN TO THE REMOTEST PART OF THE EARTH."

E.   IT STARTS WITH US, THEN IT GOES OUT TO OTHERS.

F.	Ask God to set divine appointments to share the Gospel with others. Think outward, too.

## V.	Made for miracles means we are inherently compassionate.

A.	V. 25-28 - 25 But now I am going to Jerusalem to minister to the saints. 26 For Macedonia and Achaia were pleased to make some contribution for the poor among the saints who are in Jerusalem. 27 It has pleased them indeed, and they are their debtors. For if the Gentiles have been partakers of their spiritual things, they also ought to minister to them in material things. 28 Therefore, when I have completed this and have given this blessing to them, I shall come by way of you to Spain,

B.	Miracles have inherent passion/compassion.

C.	Matthew 14:14-21 - 14 Jesus went ashore and saw a great assembly. And He was moved with compassion toward them, and He healed their sick. 15 When it was evening, His disciples came to Him, saying, "This is a lonely place and the day is now over. Send the crowds away to go into the villages and buy themselves food." 16 But Jesus said to them, "They do not need to depart. You give them something to eat." 17 They said to Him, "We have only five loaves here and two fish." 18 He said, "Bring them here to Me." 19 Then He commanded the crowds to sit down on the grass. He took the five loaves and the two fish, and looking up to heaven, He blessed and broke and gave the loaves to His disciples; and the disciples gave them to the crowds. 20 They all ate and were filled. And they took up twelve baskets full of the fragments that

REMAINED. 21 THOSE WHO HAD EATEN WERE ABOUT FIVE THOUSAND MEN, BESIDES WOMEN AND CHILDREN.

D.   MIRACLES ARE AN EXPRESSION OF GOD'S COMPASSION FOR A HURTING WORLD.

E.   ASK GOD TO HELP YOU HAVE COMPASSION FOR THE PLIGHT OF THOSE AROUND YOU.

CONCLUSION:

- Recognize that being made for miracles means that we can expect the miraculous in our lives.

21 DAYS OF HEALING
PASTOR JOHN CARMICHAEL
SESSION 14
MESSAGE TITLE: OH! NO! MY FAITH IS WEAK.

[Mat 14:29-30 NASB95] 29 And He said, "Come!" And Peter got out of the boat, and walked on the water and came toward Jesus. 30 But seeing the wind, he became frightened, and beginning to sink, he cried out, "Lord, save me!"

INTRODUCTION:

- Peter – Walking in v.29. Drowning in vs.30. "Lord, save me."
- Keith Moore talks about believing for healing and not money.
- There are areas that I am strong in faith and others that I must work on.
- What do we do? Is God mad at us? What are we to do?
- I Corinthians 14 addresses behaviors (eating, drinking, observance of special days) that come from weak or strong faith. Jesus spoke in the same manner concerning faith for miracles, healing, and the like.

Interrogative: How can we address the fact that we can be weak in faith in one area and strong in another?

Transitional: There are five ways to address the fact that we can be weak in faith in one area and strong in another.

BODY:

I. Accept yourself as God has accepted you.

A.   [ROM 14:1 NASB95] 1 NOW ACCEPT THE ONE WHO IS WEAK IN FAITH, [BUT] NOT FOR [THE PURPOSE OF] PASSING JUDGMENT ON HIS OPINIONS.

B.   WE ARE TO ACCEPT THE ONE (OTHERS AND OURSELVES) IN THIS AREA.

C.   SOMETIMES, WE CONDEMN OURSELVES AND OTHERS FOR WEAK FAITH.

D.   [ROM 14:3 NASB95] 3 THE ONE WHO EATS IS NOT TO REGARD WITH CONTEMPT THE ONE WHO DOES NOT EAT, AND THE ONE WHO DOES NOT EAT IS NOT TO JUDGE THE ONE WHO EATS, FOR GOD HAS ACCEPTED HIM.

E.   ALLOW GOD TO REMOVE THE FEAR OF REJECTION AND CONDEMNATION THAT YOU DO NOT HAVE PERFECT FAITH.

II. Acknowledge that there are levels and areas of faith.

A.   [ROM 14:1 NASB95] 1 NOW ACCEPT THE ONE WHO IS WEAK IN FAITH, [BUT] NOT FOR [THE PURPOSE OF] PASSING JUDGMENT ON HIS OPINIONS.

B.   FAITH IS NOT ONE-SIZE FITS ALL. IT IS NOT ALL-OR-NOTHING.

C.   JESUS.

1. [Mat 16:8-9 NASB95] 8 But Jesus, aware of this, said, "You men of little faith, why do you discuss among yourselves that you have no bread? 9 "Do you not yet understand or remember the five loaves of the five thousand, and how many baskets [full] you picked up?

2. [Mat 6:30 NASB95] 30 "But if God so clothes the grass of the field, which is [alive] today and tomorrow is thrown into the furnace, [will He] not much more [clothe] you? You of little faith!

3. [Mat 8:10 NASB95] 10 Now when Jesus heard [this,] He marveled and said to those who were following, "Truly I say to you, I have not found such great faith with anyone in Israel.

4. [Mat 15:28 NASB95] 28 Then Jesus said to her, "O woman, your faith is great; it shall be done for you as you wish." And her daughter was healed at once.

D.   OTHER NT WRITERS.

1. [2Th 1:3 NASB95] 3 We ought always to give thanks to God for you, brethren, as is [only] fitting, because your faith is greatly enlarged, and the love of each one of you toward one another grows [ever] greater;

2. [Act 16:5 NASB95] 5 So the churches were being strengthened in the faith, and were increasing in number daily.

E.   WHAT AREAS OF FAITH ARE YOU STRONG IN? WHAT AREAS OF FAITH ARE YOU WEAK IN?

III. Adopt a proper perspective of what God is doing in you (others).

A.   [ROM 14:17-18 NASB95] 17 FOR THE KINGDOM OF GOD IS NOT EATING AND DRINKING, BUT RIGHTEOUSNESS AND PEACE AND JOY IN THE HOLY SPIRIT. 18 FOR HE WHO IN THIS [WAY] SERVES CHRIST IS ACCEPTABLE TO GOD AND APPROVED BY MEN.

B.   WE NEED A PERSPECTIVE SHIFT NOT TO DESTROY WHAT GOD IS DOING IN OUR/OTHERS LIVES.

C.   [ROM 14:15 NASB95] 15 FOR IF BECAUSE OF FOOD YOUR BROTHER IS HURT, YOU ARE NO LONGER WALKING ACCORDING TO LOVE. DO NOT DESTROY WITH YOUR FOOD HIM FOR WHOM CHRIST DIED.

D.   WHEN WE PIGEONHOLE FAITH INTO AN ALL-OR-NOTHING MENTALITY, THEN CONDEMN OURSELVES (OR OTHERS), WE CAN DESTROY PEOPLE.

E.   SEE THE BIGGER PICTURE. WE ARE STILL WORKING ON IT. WE ARE GROWING. THERE ARE WEIGHTIER MATTERS (MATTHEW 23:23)

F.   KEEP PERSPECTIVE.

IV. Act in the faith you have only.

A.   [ROM 14:23 NASB95] 23 BUT HE WHO DOUBTS IS CONDEMNED IF HE EATS, BECAUSE [HIS EATING IS] NOT FROM FAITH; AND WHATEVER IS NOT FROM FAITH IS SIN.

B.   THIS APPLIES TO THE CURRENT CONTEXT BUT AS WE SEE FROM JESUS' WORDS, THIS APPLIES TO OTHER PLACES.

C.   SOME HAVE ASKED ABOUT WHETHER OR NOT TO GET SURGERY. DO IT OR DO NOT DO IT IN FAITH.

D.   [MAR 6:5-6 NASB95] 5 AND HE COULD DO NO MIRACLE THERE EXCEPT THAT HE LAID HIS HANDS ON A FEW SICK PEOPLE AND HEALED THEM. 6 AND HE WONDERED AT THEIR UNBELIEF. AND HE WAS GOING AROUND THE VILLAGES TEACHING.

E.   WHAT JESUS DID WAS BASED ON THEIR LEVEL OF FAITH.

F.   LEARN TO LIVE BY FAITH. ACT ON THE FAITH YOU HAVE, NOT SOMEONE ELSE'S. DO NOT FORCE SOMEONE TO WALK IN FAITH THEY DO NOT HAVE EITHER.

V.   Acquire what you need to grow in faith.

A.   [ROM 16:25-27 NASB95] 25 NOW TO HIM WHO IS ABLE TO ESTABLISH YOU ACCORDING TO MY GOSPEL AND THE PREACHING OF JESUS CHRIST, ACCORDING TO THE REVELATION OF THE MYSTERY WHICH HAS BEEN KEPT SECRET FOR LONG AGES PAST, 26 BUT NOW IS MANIFESTED, AND BY THE SCRIPTURES OF THE PROPHETS, ACCORDING TO THE COMMANDMENT OF THE ETERNAL GOD, HAS BEEN MADE KNOWN TO ALL THE NATIONS, [LEADING] TO OBEDIENCE OF FAITH; 27 TO THE ONLY WISE GOD, THROUGH JESUS CHRIST, BE THE GLORY FOREVER. AMEN.

B.   THE FACT THAT WE HAVE LEVELS OR AREAS MEANS WE CAN GROW.

C.   "GOD HAS DEALT TO EVERY PERSON A MEASURE OF FAITH (ROMANS 12:3, NKJV). BUT AS A CHRISTIAN FULL OF FAITH, GOD DOES NOT WANT YOU TO STAGNATE. HE WANTS YOU TO GROW IN HIM! GROWING IN HIM MEANS GROWING FROM FAITH TO FAITH (ROMANS 1:17, KJV). IT MEANS GETTING TO KNOW HIM BETTER AND GETTING TO KNOW HIM MORE THIS WEEK THAN LAST WEEK AND MORE TODAY THAN YESTERDAY. BELOW ARE FOUR WAYS YOU CAN GROW IN YOUR FAITH." KENNETH COPELAND

D.   THREE WAYS

1. Word - [Rom 10:17 NASB] 17 So faith [comes] from hearing, and hearing by the word of Christ.

2. Pray in Spirit - [Jde 1:20 NASB] 20 But you, beloved, building yourselves up on your most holy faith, praying in the Holy Spirit,

3. Fast - [Mat 17:21 NASB] 21 ["But this kind does not go out except by prayer and fasting."]

E.   START ACTIVELY STRENGTHENING YOUR FAITH IN AREAS.

CONCLUSION:

- Accept, Acknowledge, Adopt, Act, Acquire
- Immediately, Jesus reached out his hand and caught him. Matt. 14:30

21 DAYS OF HEALING
PASTOR JOHN CARMICHAEL
SESSION 15
MESSAGE TITLE: THE GREATEST PARABLE: HEAR & BE HEALED.

[Mar 4:13-14 NASB] 13 And He said to them, "Do you not understand this parable? How will you understand all the parables? 14 "The sower sows the word.

[Luk 5:14-16 NASB] 14 And He ordered him to tell no one, "But go and show yourself to the priest and make an offering for your cleansing, just as Moses commanded, as a testimony to them." 15 But the news about Him was spreading even farther, and large crowds were gathering to hear Him and to be healed of their sicknesses. 16 But Jesus Himself would often slip away to the wilderness and pray.

INTRODUCTION:

- Imagine a farmer expecting a harvest but not sowing seed. What would we think about that farmer? We know the laws of nature that require seed to be sown before there is a reasonable expectation of harvest.
- This parable provides a revelation of how the Kingdom of God works. The process works on a macro level as well as a micro level. It reveals how God intended to advance the Kingdom of God in general throughout the world. It reveals how God intends to advance the Kingdom of God in our individual lives.

Interrogative: How can we apply this principle of sowing the Word of God and receiving healing?

Transitional: Here are three ways to apply this principle of sowing the Word of God and receiving healing.

BODY:

I. Prescription of healing.

A.   [Pro 4:20-22 NASB] 20 MY SON, GIVE ATTENTION TO MY WORDS; INCLINE YOUR EAR TO MY SAYINGS. 21 DO NOT LET THEM DEPART FROM YOUR SIGHT; KEEP THEM IN THE MIDST OF YOUR HEART. 22 FOR THEY ARE LIFE TO THOSE WHO FIND THEM AND HEALTH TO ALL THEIR BODY.

B.   DR. GIVES YOU A PRESCRIPTION FOR MEDICINE. IT HAS HOW MANY AND HOW OFTEN. MOST PEOPLE UNDERSTAND THAT THEY MUST FOLLOW THE DOCTOR'S ORDERS TO BE HEALED.

C.   [Psa 107:20 NASB] 20 HE SENT HIS WORD AND HEALED THEM, AND DELIVERED THEM FROM THEIR DESTRUCTIONS.

D.   DECIDE TO HEAR THE WORD OF GOD.

E.   HEAR TO BE HEALED IS GOD'S PRESCRIPTION FOR RECEIVING THE HEALING JESUS PURCHASED.

II. Pattern of ministry.

A.   [Mat 4:23 NASB] 23 JESUS WAS GOING THROUGHOUT ALL GALILEE, TEACHING IN THEIR SYNAGOGUES, AND PROCLAIMING THE GOSPEL OF THE KINGDOM, AND HEALING EVERY KIND OF DISEASE AND EVERY KIND OF SICKNESS AMONG THE PEOPLE.

B.   [MAT 9:35 NASB] 35 JESUS WAS GOING THROUGH ALL THE CITIES AND VILLAGES, TEACHING IN THEIR SYNAGOGUES AND PROCLAIMING THE GOSPEL OF THE KINGDOM, AND HEALING EVERY KIND OF DISEASE AND EVERY KIND OF SICKNESS.

C.   THROUGHOUT THE HISTORY OF CHRISTIANITY, THE HEALING MINISTRY HAS BEEN PRESENT. THOUGH THE SPECIFICS MAY HAVE DIFFERED, THE BASIC PATTERN IS THE SAME: PREACHING AND HEALING IN SOME COMBINATION. MARIA WOODSWORTH ETTER (INDIANAPOLIS, IN). WILLIAM BRANHAM (JEFFERSONVILLE, IN)

D.   [LUK 6:17-19 NASB] 17 JESUS CAME DOWN WITH THEM AND STOOD ON A LEVEL PLACE; AND THERE WAS A LARGE CROWD OF HIS DISCIPLES, AND A GREAT THRONG OF PEOPLE FROM ALL JUDEA AND JERUSALEM AND THE COASTAL REGION OF TYRE AND SIDON, 18 WHO HAD COME TO HEAR HIM AND TO BE HEALED OF THEIR DISEASES; AND THOSE WHO WERE TROUBLED WITH UNCLEAN SPIRITS WERE BEING CURED. 19 AND ALL THE PEOPLE WERE TRYING TO TOUCH HIM, FOR POWER WAS COMING FROM HIM AND HEALING THEM ALL.

E.   DO NOT DIMINISH THIS PATTERN.

F.   FOLLOW AND SUBMIT TO THE PATTERN OF RECEIVING HEALING MINISTRY.

G.   G. HEAR TO BE HEALED IS THE PATTERN OF JESUS' & THE CHURCH'S MINISTRY TO RECEIVING THE HEALING JESUS' PURCHASED.

III. Priority of hearing.

A.   [Mar 4:24 NASB] 24 And He was saying to them, "Take care what you listen to. By your standard of measure it will be measured to you; and more will be given you besides.

B.   Mark 4:24 And He said to them, Be careful what you are hearing. The measure [a][of thought and study] you give [to [b]the truth you hear] will be the measure [c] [of virtue and knowledge] that comes back to you—and more [besides] will be given to you who hear.

C.   Not earplugs to hear nothing. But isolation headphones to hear what you want/need to hear.

D.   Be careful. It is hard to hear more than one thing at a time.

E.   Sometimes, you must tune things out and focus only on what you want to hear.

F.   Hear and be healed takes planning and discernment to receive the healing Jesus purchased.

CONCLUSION:

- [Act 14:8-10 NASB] 8 At Lystra a man was sitting who had no strength in his feet, lame from his mother's womb, who had never walked. 9 This man was listening to Paul as he spoke, who, when he had fixed his gaze on him and had seen that he had faith to be made well, 10 said with a loud voice, "Stand upright on your feet." And he leaped up and began to walk.

- This man followed the prescription. He was listening.
- This man submitted to the pattern. He listened and stood up.
- This man prioritized hearing. He overcame "you can't come" "it will be too hard to get to the meeting to hear." (How much planning did it take to get the lame man to the meeting?) He did not listen to why he could not walk. He listened to why he could.
- Read, hear, obey, and believe the Word of God.
- Understand it is working healing in you.
- Spend time in God's Word, even in your thinking.

21 DAYS OF HEALING
PASTOR JOHN CARMICHAEL
SESSION 16
MESSAGE TITLE: MADE WHOLE: REPROGRAMMED.

Romans 12:1-2 NASB1 Therefore I urge you, brethren, by the mercies of God, to present your bodies a living and holy sacrifice, acceptable to God, which is your spiritual service of worship. 2 And do not be conformed to this world, but be transformed by the renewing of your mind, so that you may prove what the will of God is, that which is good and acceptable and perfect.

INTRODUCTION:

- Due to sin, our mind starts off as a malfunctioning computer. When we become born again, God gives us the mind of Christ. Yet, we must develop or reprogram our minds to cooperate with the mind He has placed in us.
- The Apostle Paul spends much of the book of Romans teaching doctrine. Chapter 12, he helps them to apply what he taught.
- In Romans 12:1-2, we see how to develop into believers God wants us to become.

Interrogative: What are the main aspects of the mind renewal process from this passage?

Transitional: There are three (3) main aspects of the mind renewal process.

BODY:

I. Apply God's Word to your life.

A.　　VERSE 1A: THEREFORE, I URGE YOU, BRETHREN, BY THE MERCIES OF GOD,

B.　　THEREFORE . . .

1. Adam Clark says chapter leaves the theology and begins the practical.

2. Principle vs. practical. Academic vs. application. Theology vs. relatable. What I need to know vs. what I need to do. We need to get the truth out of the church and into the kitchen, out of the sanctuary, and into the bedroom.

3. [Jas 1:22-25 NASB] 22 But prove yourselves doers of the word, and not merely hearers who delude themselves. 23 For if anyone is a hearer of the word and not a doer, he is like a man who looks at his natural face in a mirror; 24 for once he has looked at himself and gone away, he has immediately forgotten what kind of person he was. 25 But one who looks intently at the perfect law, the law of liberty, and abides by it, not having become a forgetful hearer but an effectual doer, this man will be blessed in what he does.

4. Apply what you hear!

C.　　. . . I URGE YOU . . .

1. Speaks of importance.

2. The games we play with God's Word and our walk with Him has to stop.

D.   . . . Brethren. . .

1. Jews and Gentiles were there.

2. Oxymoron: It is for everyone individually.

E.   . . . By the mercies of God . . .

1. Understanding it is more about what He did than what we do.

2. We are dependent upon Him every step of the way.

II.   . . . Present yourself to God wholly . . .

A.   Verse 1b: to present your bodies a living and holy sacrifice acceptable to God, which is your spiritual service of worship.

B.   Present your bodies . . .

1. 1. Requires action. Requires decision.

2. Giving God the right to be the LORD of your life.

C.   . . . Living and holy sacrifice . . .

1. Living is your do.

2. Holy is you who.

... Acceptable to God ...

1. This is what God is thinks is acceptable.

2. [Mic 6:8 NASB] 8 He has told you, O man, what is good; And what does the LORD require of you But to do justice, to love kindness, And to walk humbly with your God?

D.   ... WHICH IS YOUR SPIRITUAL SERVICE OF WORSHIP ...

1. Spiritual is also translated as rational.

2. Apostle Paul describes what real Christianity looks like.

III. Prove (approve) of God's Will for your life.

A.   VERSE 2: AND DO NOT BE CONFORMED TO THIS WORLD, BUT BE TRANSFORMED BY THE RENEWING OF YOUR MIND, SO THAT YOU MAY PROVE WHAT THE WILL OF GOD IS, THAT WHICH IS GOOD AND ACCEPTABLE AND PERFECT.

B.   DO NOT BE CONFORMED TO THIS WORLD (AGE)

1. Come out of the mold (the image) the world wants us to be in. Look different.

2. [1Pe 2:9-10 NASB] 9 But you are A CHOSEN RACE, A royal PRIESTHOOD, A HOLY NATION, A PEOPLE FOR God's OWN POSSESSION, so that you may proclaim the excellencies of Him who has called you out of darkness into His marvelous light; 10 for you once were NOT A PEOPLE, but now you are

THE PEOPLE OF GOD; you had NOT RECEIVED MERCY, but now you have RECEIVED MERCY.

C.   . . . BE TRANSFORMED . . .

1. New information. A new way of life.

2. God is anointing you to be transformed. You are going to be different.

D.   . . . BY THE RENEWING OF YOUR MIND . . .

1. This speaks to process.

2. [Col 3:2 NASB] 2 Set your mind on the things above, not on the things that are on earth.

3. [Jos 1:8 NASB] 8 "This book of the law shall not depart from your mouth, but you shall meditate on it day and night, so that you may be careful to do according to all that is written in it; for then you will make your way prosperous, and then you will have success.

4. [Psa 1:2-3 NASB] 2 But his delight is in the law of the LORD, And in His law he meditates day and night. 3 He will be like a tree firmly planted by streams of water, Which yields its fruit in its season And its leaf does not wither; And in whatever he does, he prospers.

5. [Mark 4:24 (AMPC)] - And He said to them, Be careful what you are hearing. The measure [of thought and study] you give [to the truth you hear] will be the measure [of virtue and knowledge]

that comes back to you—and more [besides] will be given to you who hear.

E.   . . . So that you may prove what the will of God is . . .

1. Prove (approve). Know. Discern.

2. Come into agreement with what God has for you.

3. You are going to experience God's Will for your life!

F.   . . . That which is . . .

1. . . . Good . . .

a. Honorable, joyful, and pleasant.

b. [Mat 7:11 NASB] 11 "If you then, being evil, know how to give good gifts to your children, how much more will your Father who is in heaven give what is good to those who ask Him!

c. God has good for you!

2. . . . Acceptable . . .

a. Well pleasing.

b.   [Psa 37:23 NASB] 23 The steps of a man are established by the LORD, And He delights in his way.

3. . . . Perfect . . .

a. Complete and mature.

b. [1Pe 5:10 NASB] 10 After you have suffered for a little while, the God of all grace, who called you to His eternal glory in Christ, will Himself perfect, confirm, strengthen, and establish you.

CONCLUSION:

- Decide to apply what you learn from God's Word to your everyday life.
- Surrender your life and attitude to God's ways. Allow Him to help you.
- Expect to experience God's Will… it is good, acceptable, and perfect.
- Understand the mind renewal process. Surrender to Him. Commit to reading, studying, and meditating on God's Word.

21 DAYS OF HEALING
PASTOR JOHN CARMICHAEL
SESSION 17
MESSAGE TITLE: MADE WHOLE: TOTAL HEALING.

[Isa 53:1-6 NASB] 1 Who has believed our message? And to whom has the arm of the LORD been revealed? 2 For He grew up before Him like a tender shoot, And like a root out of parched ground; He has no stately form or majesty That we should look upon Him, Nor appearance that we should be attracted to Him. 3 He was despised and forsaken of men, A man of sorrows and acquainted with grief; And like one from whom men hide their face He was despised, and we did not esteem Him. 4 Surely our griefs He Himself bore, And our sorrows He carried; Yet we ourselves esteemed Him stricken, Smitten of God, and afflicted. 5 But He was pierced through for our transgressions, He was crushed for our iniquities; The chastening for our well-being fell upon Him, And by His scourging we are healed. 6 All of us like sheep have gone astray, Each of us has turned to his own way; But the LORD has caused the iniquity of us all To fall on Him.

Message: Adam's sin resulted in a total wreck of humanity, while Jesus' sacrifice resulted in a total healing of humanity.

Response: Release faith for the total healing of their entire being.

INTRODUCTION

- The call came as a surprise. For some odd reason, I thought JJ was joking. He was not joking. (Describe the accident of the truck.) The car he hit was totaled. It was beyond repair. Thank God no one was injured. The man in the totaled car got a new car. I am not sure how it worked.

- When Adam fell in the Garden, it was an act that totally wrecked humankind.
- In Isaiah 53, we get a description of how God showed up to the wreck of humankind that totaled us with the payment to become new.
- "Totaled" shows us the enormity of the wreck. It also brings the promise of total replacement.

Interrogative: How did Christ overcome the effects of the brokenness of our lives? What should we do to receive the payment for total healing? How can we have confidence in the completeness of Christ's wholeness for us?

Transitional: There are four (4) aspects of the total healing Christ has for us.

I.   First, God's report and power must be received by us.

A.   A.   In v.1, Who has believed our message? And to whom has the arm of the LORD been revealed?

B.   B.   Do you know your coverage? Have you read your policy? Is the company capable of the payout?

C.   C. Two major questions to receiving total healing.

1. A report to be believed.

2. An Arm to be revealed.

D.   MATTHEW 22:29 - [MAT 22:29 NASB] 29 BUT JESUS ANSWERED AND SAID TO THEM, "YOU ARE MISTAKEN, NOT UNDERSTANDING THE SCRIPTURES NOR THE POWER OF GOD.

E.   READ, STUDY, AND UNDERSTAND THE SCRIPTURE AND BUILD FAITH IN GOD'S POWER.

F.   SAY, "GOD'S WORD AND POWER IS ENOUGH TO HEAL ME TOTALLY!"

II. Second, God identifies with us.

A.   IN V. 2-3, 2 FOR HE GREW UP BEFORE HIM LIKE A TENDER SHOOT, AND LIKE A ROOT OUT OF PARCHED GROUND; HE HAS NO STATELY FORM OR MAJESTY THAT WE SHOULD LOOK UPON HIM, NOR APPEARANCE THAT WE SHOULD BE ATTRACTED TO HIM. 3 HE WAS DESPISED AND FORSAKEN OF MEN, A MAN OF SORROWS AND ACQUAINTED WITH GRIEF; AND LIKE ONE FROM WHOM MEN HIDE THEIR FACE HE WAS DESPISED, AND WE DID NOT ESTEEM HIM.

B.   INSURANCE COMPANIES TEST WRECKS AND KNOW THE COST DOWN TO PENNIES.

C.   DON STEWART - BECAUSE JESUS, THE GOD-MAN, LIVED HERE ON THE EARTH AND EXPERIENCED THE LIMITATIONS OF BEING A HUMAN BEING, HE CAN SYMPATHIZE WITH THE PROBLEMS AND CONCERNS THAT HUMANS FACE.

D.   HEBREWS 4:14-16 THEREFORE, SINCE WE HAVE A GREAT HIGH PRIEST WHO HAS GONE THROUGH THE HEAVENS, JESUS THE SON OF GOD, LET US HOLD FIRMLY TO THE FAITH WE

PROFESS. FOR WE DO NOT HAVE A HIGH PRIEST WHO IS UNABLE TO SYMPATHIZE WITH OUR WEAKNESSES, BUT WE HAVE ONE WHO HAS BEEN TEMPTED IN EVERY WAY, JUST AS WE ARE - YET WAS WITHOUT SIN. LET US THEN APPROACH THE THRONE OF GRACE WITH CONFIDENCE, SO THAT WE MAY RECEIVE MERCY AND FIND GRACE TO HELP US IN OUR TIME OF NEED (HEBREWS 4:14-16).

E. TO TOTALLY HEAL US, HE HAD TO BECOME TOTALLY ONE OF US.

F. JESUS KNOWS WHAT BROKENNESS IS LIKE.

III. Thirdly, God did it for us.

A. IN V. 4, SURELY OUR GRIEFS HE HIMSELF BORE, AND OUR SORROWS HE CARRIED; YET WE OURSELVES ESTEEMED HIM STRICKEN, SMITTEN OF GOD, AND AFFLICTED.

B. MY SON PAID THE POLICY. THE OTHER MAN GOT A NEW CAR. THE METAPHOR BREAKS DOWN A LITTLE HERE.

C. "BORE" & "CARRIED" - SAME WORDS AS IN V. 11

D. "GRIEFS" & "SORROWS" SPECIFICALLY MEAN PHYSICAL AFFLICTION (SEE MATT. 8:17)

E. [2CO 5:19, 21 NASB] 19 NAMELY, THAT GOD WAS IN CHRIST RECONCILING THE WORLD TO HIMSELF, NOT COUNTING THEIR TRESPASSES AGAINST THEM, AND HE HAS COMMITTED TO US THE WORD OF RECONCILIATION. ... 21 HE MADE HIM WHO KNEW NO SIN TO BE SIN ON OUR BEHALF, SO THAT WE MIGHT BECOME THE RIGHTEOUSNESS OF GOD IN HIM.

F.   GOD DID NOT DO IT TO HIM. OUR SIN DID. GOD RESPONDED TO HIM BASED ON OUR SINS.

G.   IT WAS A GREAT EXCHANGE. WE GOT THE TOTALITY OF HIS WHOLENESS, AND HE TOOK THE TOTALITY OF OUR BROKENNESS.

IV. Fourthly, God heals ALL (totally) of us.

A.   IN V. 5, BUT HE WAS PIERCED THROUGH FOR OUR TRANSGRESSIONS, HE WAS CRUSHED FOR OUR INIQUITIES; THE CHASTENING FOR OUR WELL-BEING FELL UPON HIM, AND BY HIS SCOURGING WE ARE HEALED.

B.   ONCE ASSESSED AS A TOTAL LOSS, IT REQUIRED A TOTAL REPLACEMENT.

C.   [1TH 5:23 NASB] 23 NOW MAY THE GOD OF PEACE HIMSELF SANCTIFY YOU ENTIRELY; AND MAY YOUR SPIRIT AND SOUL AND BODY BE PRESERVED COMPLETE, WITHOUT BLAME AT THE COMING OF OUR LORD JESUS CHRIST.

D.   THE TOTAL PACKAGE.

1. Transgression and iniquities is spiritual wounds. Matt. 27:46 – "My God, My God . . . forsake Me?"

2. Well-being (peace) is soul wounds. Luke 22:44 – "anguish . . . drops of blood . . ."

3. Healing is physical wounds. I Peter 3:18 – ". . . put to death in the flesh . . ."

a. Matthew 8:17 - [Mat 8:17 NASB] 17 This was to fulfill what was spoken through Isaiah the prophet: "HE HIMSELF TOOK OUR INFIRMITIES AND CARRIED AWAY OUR DISEASES."

b. Matthew 12:14-17 - [Mat 12:14-17 NASB] 14 But the Pharisees went out and conspired against Him, as to how they might destroy Him. 15 But Jesus, aware of this, withdrew from there. Many followed Him, and He healed them all, 16 and warned them not to tell who He was. 17 This was to fulfill what was spoken through Isaiah the prophet:

CONCLUSION:

- Humanity was a total wreck.
- Jesus' atonement was for total healing!

21 DAYS OF HEALING
PASTOR JOHN CARMICHAEL
SESSION 18
MESSAGE TITLE: MADE WHOLE: LEGENDARY TOUCH

[Mat 9:20-22 NASB] 20 And a woman who had been suffering from a hemorrhage for twelve years, came up behind Him and touched the fringe of His cloak; 21 for she was saying to herself, "If I only touch His garment, I will get well." 22 But Jesus turning and seeing her said, "Daughter, take courage; your faith has made you well." At once the woman was made well.

[Mar 5:25-34 NASB] 25 A woman who had had a hemorrhage for twelve years, 26 and had endured much at the hands of many physicians, and had spent all that she had and was not helped at all, but rather had grown worse-- 27 after hearing about Jesus, she came up in the crowd behind Him and touched His cloak. 28 For she thought, "If I just touch His garments, I will get well." 29 Immediately the flow of her blood was dried up; and she felt in her body that she was healed of her affliction. 30 Immediately Jesus, perceiving in Himself that the power proceeding from Him had gone forth, turned around in the crowd and said, "Who touched My garments?" 31 And His disciples said to Him, "You see the crowd pressing in on You, and You say, 'Who touched Me?'" 32 And He looked around to see the woman who had done this. 33 But the woman fearing and trembling, aware of what had happened to her, came, and fell down before Him and told Him the whole truth. 34 And He said to her, "Daughter, your faith has made you well; go in peace and be healed of your affliction."

[Luk 8:43-48 NASB] 43 And a woman who had a hemorrhage for twelve years, and could not be healed by anyone, 44 came up behind Him and touched the fringe of His cloak, and immediately her hemorrhage stopped. 45 And Jesus said, "Who is the one who touched Me?" And while they were all denying it, Peter said, "Master, the people are crowding and pressing in on You." 46 But Jesus said, "Someone did touch Me, for I was aware that power had gone out of Me."

47 When the woman saw that she had not escaped notice, she came trembling and fell down before Him, and declared in the presence of all the people the reason why she had touched Him, and how she had been immediately healed. 48 And He said to her, "Daughter, your faith has made you well; go in peace."

INTRODUCTION:

- This sick, anonymous woman must have been emaciated after a hemorrhage lasting for twelve years, which rendered her legally unclean. She could not throw herself, therefore, at the feet of Christ and state her complaint. Her modesty, humility, uncleanness, and pressure of the crowd made close contact well-nigh impossible, hence her eagerness to touch in some unnoticed way the hem of His garment. Who was this woman of faith? The primitive church, feeling she was entitled to a name, called her Veronica, who lived in Caesarea Philippi, but in the gospels she is enrolled in the list of anonymous female divines. (Source: ALL THE WOMEN OF THE BIBLE – WOMAN WITH ISSUE OF BLOOD)
- Her name might not be mentioned, but her legendary touch faith was in (3) of the Gospels.

Interrogative: What does a "legendary touch" for wholeness look like?

Transitional: Here are seven attributes of a "legendary touch" that we can incorporate in our lives as we seek healing.

BODY:

I.   Legendary touch starts with a destitute condition.

A.   12 YEARS ISSUE OF BLOOD

B.   SPENT ALL SHE HAD, SUFFERED AT THE HANDS OF MANY PHYSICIANS — WORSE!

II. Legendary touch receives a glorious report

A.   MARK 5:27 — SHE HEARD ABOUT JESUS.

B.   SOMEBODY TOLD HER ABOUT JESUS.

C.   SHE BELIEVED WHAT SHE WAS TOLD ABOUT JESUS.

III. Legendary touch makes a marvelous confession.

A.   MATTHEW 9:21 — SHE WAS SAYING TO HERSELF.

B.   MARK 5:28 — FOR SHE THOUGHT.

IV. Legendary touch takes courageous action

A.   MATTHEW 9:20 — CAME UP BEHIND HIM AND TOUCHED THE FRINGE OF CLOAK.

B.   MARK 5:27 - SHE CAME UP INTO THE CROWD BEHIND HIM AND TOUCHED HIS CLOAK.

C.   LUKE 8:44 - CAME UP BEHIND HIM AND TOUCHED THE FRINGE OF HIS CLOAK.

V. Legendary touch experiences an immediate response.

A.   A DIVINE REACTION.

1. Mark 5:30 Immediately Jesus, perceiving in Himself that the power proceeding from Him had gone forth, turned around in the crowd and said, "Who touched My garments?" 31 And His disciples said to Him, "You see the crowd pressing in on You, and You say, 'Who touched Me?'"

2. Luke 8:45 And Jesus said, "Who is the one who touched Me?" And while they were all denying it, Peter said, "Master, the people are crowding and pressing in on You." 46 But Jesus said, "Someone did touch Me, for I was aware that power had gone out of Me."

B.   A EARTHLY RESULT.

1.   Mark 5:29 Immediately the flow of her blood was dried up; and she felt in her body that she was healed of her affliction.

2.   Luke 8:44 - and immediately, her hemorrhage stopped.

VI. Legendary touch is given favorable recognition.

A.   MATTHEW 9:22 BUT JESUS TURNING AND SEEING HER SAID, "DAUGHTER, TAKE COURAGE;

B.   MARK 5:32 AND HE LOOKED AROUND TO SEE THE WOMAN WHO HAD DONE THIS. 33 BUT THE WOMAN FEARING AND TREMBLING, AWARE OF WHAT HAD HAPPENED TO HER, CAME, AND FELL DOWN BEFORE HIM AND TOLD HIM THE WHOLE TRUTH. 34 AND HE SAID TO HER, "DAUGHTER, YOUR FAITH HAS MADE YOU WELL; GO IN PEACE AND BE HEALED OF YOUR AFFLICTION."

C.   LUKE 8: 47 WHEN THE WOMAN SAW THAT SHE HAD NOT ESCAPED NOTICE, SHE CAME TREMBLING AND FELL DOWN BEFORE HIM, AND DECLARED IN THE PRESENCE OF ALL THE PEO-

PLE THE REASON WHY SHE HAD TOUCHED HIM, AND HOW SHE HAD BEEN IMMEDIATELY HEALED. 48 AND HE SAID TO HER, "DAUGH-TER,..."

VII. Legendary touch has an eternal truth.

A.   MATTHEW 9:22 - YOUR FAITH HAS MADE YOU WELL."

B.   MARK 5:34 AND HE SAID TO HER, "DAUGHTER, YOUR FAITH HAS MADE YOU WELL; GO IN PEACE AND BE HEALED OF YOUR AFFLICTION."

C.   LUKE 8:48 AND HE SAID TO HER, "DAUGHTER, YOUR FAITH HAS MADE YOU WELL; GO IN PEACE."

CONCLUSION

- About AD320, Eusebius, Bishop of Caesarea and a dependable historian, records that when he visited Caesarea Philippi, he heard that the woman healed of her issue of blood out of gratitude for her cure had erected two brazen figures at the gate of her house, one representing a woman bending on her knee in supplication—the other, fashioned in the likeness of Jesus, holding out His hand to help her. The figure had a double cloak of brass. Eusebius adds this explicit statement as to these figures, "They were in existence even in our day, and we saw them with our own eyes when we stayed in the city."

21 DAYS OF HEALING
PASTOR JOHN CARMICHAEL
SESSION 19
MESSAGE TITLE: WHAT IS THE PURPOSE OF HEALING MIRA-CLES?

[Jhn 5:19 NASB95] 19 Therefore Jesus answered and was saying to them, "Truly, truly, I say to you, the Son can do nothing of Himself, unless [it is] something He sees the Father doing; for whatever the Father does, these things the Son also does in like manner.

INTRODUCTION

- Jesus is the embodiment of the Will of God. Everything Jesus did was God's Will.

Interrogative: Why does the fact that Jesus only did God's Will on earth affect our faith to be healed?

Transitional: If we learn the purpose of Jesus' Healing Miracle Ministry, we can know the purpose today.

BODY:

I. Jesus loves humans.

A.   A. MATTHEW 9:35 JESUS WAS GOING THROUGH ALL THE CITIES AND VILLAGES, TEACHING IN THEIR SYNAGOGUES AND PROCLAIMING THE GOSPEL OF THE KINGDOM, AND HEALING EVERY KIND OF DISEASE AND EVERY KIND OF SICKNESS. 36 SEEING THE [AB]PEOPLE, HE FELT COMPASSION FOR THEM, BECAUSE THEY WERE [AC]DISTRESSED AND [AD]DISPIRITED LIKE SHEEP [AE]WITHOUT

A SHEPHERD. 37 THEN HE *SAID TO HIS DISCIPLES, "THE HAR-
VEST IS PLENTIFUL, BUT THE WORKERS ARE FEW. 38 THEREFORE
BESEECH THE LORD OF THE HARVEST TO SEND OUT WORKERS INTO
HIS HARVEST."

B.   B. MATTHEW 14:14 - WHEN HE WENT [H]ASHORE,
HE SAW A LARGE CROWD, AND FELT COMPASSION FOR THEM AND
HEALED THEIR SICK.

C.   C.   HE HAS COMPASSION FOR THE MISERY HUMANS GO
THROUGH DUE TO THE FALL. HE DID NOT INTEND FOR HUMANS TO
DEAL WITH SICKNESS.

D.   D.   JESUS' RESPONSE IN HEALING THOSE SICK MANI-
FEST GOD'S CONCERN FOR ALL THOSE WHO SUFFER. IT ALSO SHOWS
THAT IN HIS KINGLY REIGN, THERE IS THE POWER TO OVERCOME
SUFFERING.

E.   E.   WHEN HIS DEAR FRIEND LAZARUS DIED, JESUS
WEPT AS HE STOOD OUTSIDE THE GRAVE. THE GOSPEL WRITER
JOHN TELLS US THIS: "JESUS WAS DEEPLY MOVED IN SPIRIT AND
TROUBLED" (JOHN 11: 33). IN GREEK, THESE WORDS ARE UNUSU-
ALLY INTENSE. THEY COULD ALSO BE TRANSLATED: 'JESUS WAS
ENRAGED IN SPIRIT AND TROUBLED.' IN OTHER WORDS, JESUS WAS
REALLY ANGRY AT DEATH. HE WAS ANGRY AT THE HORROR OF
DEATH, WHICH CAUSED SO MUCH PAIN AND ANGUISH THROUGHOUT
OUR LIVES. HE WAS ANGRY AT HOW DEATH DESTROYS RELATION-
SHIPS AND SNUFFS OUT THE PROMISE OF LIFE. HE WAS ANGRY THAT
DEATH HAD HAPPENED AT ALL.

II. Jesus hates Satan.

A.   ACTS 10:38 - YOU KNOW OF JESUS OF NAZARETH, HOW GOD ANOINTED HIM WITH THE HOLY SPIRIT AND WITH POWER, AND HOW HE WENT ABOUT DOING GOOD AND HEALING ALL WHO WERE OPPRESSED BY THE DEVIL, FOR GOD WAS WITH HIM.

B.   LUKE 13:16 - AND THIS WOMAN, A DAUGHTER OF ABRAHAM AS SHE IS, WHOM SATAN HAS BOUND FOR EIGHTEEN LONG YEARS, SHOULD SHE NOT HAVE BEEN RELEASED FROM THIS BOND ON THE SABBATH DAY?"

C.   HIS HEALING MINISTRY OVERTHROWS THE HORRIBLE ATTACKS OF SICKNESS SATAN USES AGAINST GOD'S BELOVED.

D.   DEMON POSSESSION IS A FREQUENT OCCURRENCE IN THE GOSPEL ACCOUNTS. THE VERY PRESENCE OF JESUS PROVOKED FIERCE HOSTILITY FROM THE DEVIL. SOME MODERN SCHOLARS CLAIM THAT PEOPLE IN THE FIRST CENTURY SUPERSTITIOUSLY ASSOCIATED ILLNESS AND INSANITY WITH DEMON POSSESSION. BUT IN FACT, THE GOSPEL WRITERS DID NOT SEE A DEMON BEHIND EVERY ILLNESS. LUKE WAS A DOCTOR WHO DIFFERENTIATED BETWEEN DEMON POSSESSION AND PHYSICAL SICKNESS OR MENTAL DISEASE.

E.   SO, WHAT IS DEMON POSSESSION? THE GOSPEL WRITERS SAY THAT THOSE WHOSE PERSONALITIES HAD BEEN TAKEN OVER BY DEMONS WERE POSSESSED. SOMETIMES THEY HAD NO CONTROL OVER THEIR WORDS OR ACTIONS. IN A FEW CASES, DEMON POSSESSION WAS A CAUSE OF DUMBNESS OR EPILEPSY. OF COURSE, THE BIBLE IS NOT TEACHING THAT DEMONS CAUSE ALL OR EVEN MOST DUMBNESS OR EPILEPSY. NONETHELESS, WHEN JESUS WAS DELIVERING PEOPLE FROM THIS TERRIBLE CONDITION, HE WAS ATTACKING

THE SOURCE OF MUCH OF THE SUFFERING AND EVIL IN THE WORLD: THE DEVIL AND HIS MINIONS.

III. Jesus displays Himself.

A.   A THIRD REASON JESUS WORKED MIRACLES IS MENTIONED IN THE GOSPEL OF JOHN: "JESUS PERFORMED MANY OTHER SIGNS IN THE PRESENCE OF HIS DISCIPLES, WHICH ARE NOT RECORDED IN THIS BOOK. BUT THESE ARE WRITTEN THAT YOU MAY BELIEVE THAT JESUS IS THE MESSIAH, THE SON OF GOD AND THAT BY BELIEVING, YOU MAY HAVE LIFE IN HIS NAME (20:30, 31)." THAT IS TO SAY, THE MIRACLES SERVED AS SIGNPOSTS, POINTING TO WHO JESUS WAS SO THAT PEOPLE WOULD COME TO FAITH IN HIM.

B.   HE DISPLAYS HIMSELF AS THE ANSWER TO SIN, SICKNESS, AND SATAN. THE HEALING MIRACLES SERVE AS SIGNPOSTS THAT JESUS CHRIST IS THE MESSIAH. HE IS THE SACRIFICIAL CURE TO ALL THE ILLS OF HUMANITY.

C.   FOR EXAMPLE, MATTHEW TELLS US: "ONE DAY SOME TEACHERS OF RELIGIOUS LAW AND PHARISEES CAME TO JESUS AND SAID, 'TEACHER, WE WANT YOU TO SHOW US A MIRACULOUS SIGN TO PROVE YOUR AUTHORITY. 'HE ANSWERED, 'ONLY AN EVIL AND ADULTEROUS GENERATION WOULD DEMAND A MIRACULOUS SIGN!'" (12:38, 39, NEW LIVING TRANSLATION)

D.   THERE IS A DANGER TODAY THAT WE CAN FOCUS MORE ON THE MIRACLES THAN ON THE MIRACLE-WORKING GOD. WE WANT THE PENNIES IN JESUS' HAND, BUT WE DO NOT WANT TO TAKE HIS HAND OR HAVE HIM TAKE OUR HAND AND LEAD US. WE DO NOT WANT HIM AT THE CENTER OF OUR LIVES AND VALUE SYSTEMS.

IV. Jesus teaches the disciples how to minister.

A.   JOHN 14:11 BELIEVE ME THAT I AM IN THE FATHER AND THE FATHER IS IN ME; OTHERWISE BELIEVE BECAUSE OF THE WORKS THEMSELVES. 12 TRULY, TRULY, I SAY TO YOU, HE WHO BELIEVES IN ME, THE WORKS THAT I DO, HE WILL DO ALSO; AND GREATER WORKS THAN THESE HE WILL DO; BECAUSE I GO TO THE FATHER.

B.   MATTHEW 10:7 AND AS YOU GO, [H]PREACH, SAYING, 'THE KINGDOM OF HEAVEN [I]IS AT HAND.' 8 HEAL THE SICK, RAISE THE DEAD, CLEANSE THE LEPERS, CAST OUT DEMONS. FREELY YOU RECEIVED, FREELY GIVE. 9 DO NOT ACQUIRE GOLD, OR SILVER, OR COPPER FOR YOUR MONEY BELTS, 10 OR A [J]BAG FOR YOUR JOURNEY, OR EVEN TWO [K]COATS, OR SANDALS, OR A STAFF; FOR THE WORKER IS WORTHY OF HIS [L]SUPPORT. 11 AND WHATEVER CITY OR VILLAGE YOU ENTER, INQUIRE WHO IS WORTHY IN IT, AND STAY [M]AT HIS HOUSE UNTIL YOU LEAVE THAT CITY. 12 AS YOU ENTER THE [N]HOUSE, GIVE IT YOUR GREETING. 13 IF THE HOUSE IS WORTHY, GIVE IT YOUR BLESSING OF PEACE. BUT IF IT IS NOT WORTHY, [Q]TAKE BACK YOUR BLESSING OF PEACE. 14 WHOEVER DOES NOT RECEIVE YOU, NOR HEED YOUR WORDS, AS YOU GO OUT OF THAT HOUSE OR THAT CITY, SHAKE THE DUST OFF YOUR FEET. 15 TRULY I SAY TO YOU, IT WILL BE MORE TOLERABLE FOR THE LAND OF SODOM AND GOMORRAH IN THE DAY OF JUDGMENT THAN FOR THAT CITY.

C.   MARK 16 – WHOEVER BELIEVES.

V. Jesus teaches the sick how to receive.

A. 2 TIMOTHY 3:16 ALL SCRIPTURE IS [H]INSPIRED BY GOD AND PROFITABLE FOR TEACHING, FOR REPROOF, FOR CORRECTION, FOR [I]TRAINING IN RIGHTEOUSNESS; 17 SO THAT THE MAN OF GOD MAY BE ADEQUATE, EQUIPPED FOR EVERY GOOD WORK.

B. ACTS 10:34 OPENING HIS MOUTH, PETER SAID: "I MOST CERTAINLY UNDERSTAND NOW THAT GOD IS NOT ONE TO SHOW PARTIALITY, 35 BUT IN EVERY NATION THE MAN WHO [Y] FEARS HIM AND [Z]DOES WHAT IS RIGHT IS WELCOME TO HIM.

C. ROMANS 2:11 - 11 FOR THERE IS NO PARTIALITY WITH GOD.

D. WHAT GOD DOES FOR ONE, HE DOES FOR ALL.

CONCLUSION:

- Jesus' purposes should be ours.
- Note: the reaction we get will be similar too.
- John 11:45 - 45 Therefore many of the Jews who came to Mary, and saw what He had done, believed in Him. 46 But some of them went to the Pharisees and told them the things which Jesus had done.
- We are to be healed and pray for healing because Jesus said to.
- Mark 16 - 15 And He said to them, "Go into all the world and preach the gospel to all creation. 16 He who has believed and has been baptized shall be saved; but he who has disbelieved shall be condemned. 17 These

[d]signs will accompany those who have believed: in
My name they will cast out demons, they will speak
with new tongues; 18 they will pick up serpents, and if
they drink any deadly poison, it will not hurt them; they
will lay hands on the sick, and they will recover." 19 So
then, when the Lord Jesus had spoken to them, He was
received up into heaven and sat down at the right hand
of God. 20 And they went out and preached everywhere, while the Lord worked with them, and confirmed
the word by the [e]signs that followed.]

21 DAYS OF HEALING
PASTOR JOHN CARMICHAEL
SESSION 20
MESSAGE TITLE: EVEN NOW: FAITH THAT ENDURES

[Jhn 11:21-22 NASB95] 21 Martha then said to Jesus, "Lord, if You had been here, my brother would not have died. 22 "Even now I know that whatever You ask of God, God will give You."

INTRODUCTION:

- Recap the story
- Martha makes two confessions of faith: 1. If you had been here; 2. Even now…
- Two levels of faith. One is good. The other is better.
- "Even now" faith endures every trial and circumstance

Interrogative: What does "even now" faith look like?

Transitional: We need to understand what "even now" faith does and does not look like.

BODY:

I.   Even Now faith is not based on:

A.   TIME - V. 6 & 21 - "TOO LONG", "IF HE WAS GOING TO DO ANYTHING, HE WOULD HAVE ALREADY DONE IT."

1. We expect v. 6 to read He came

2. He waited. Sometimes He waits.

3. Hebrews 11 shows many times He waits.

4. Faith based on time is weak faith.

B.   CIRCUMSTANCE - V. 14, 21

1. Egg Hunts. The bad weather of an egg hunt in Clinton, KY still had a good result.

2. Circumstance says God can only work "this way." God can perform His promises in any situation.

3. God ignores deadlines.

II.   Even Now IS Based

A.   UNDERSTANDING HIS PASSION V.5

1. Martha had faith in Him because she knew He loved her.

2. Only when we are convinced of His love for us will "Even Now" faith be with us.

B.   B. UNDERSTANDING HIS POSITION V.27

1. Lord - She had a personal relationship with Him.

2. Be a seeker before you are a speaker.

3. Result or Relationship.

4. When He is Lord, the faith principles take on a whole new form.

C.   C. UNDERSTANDING HIS PURPOSE V.27

1.   Christ - He came to seek and save that which was lost

2.   Anointed One and His anointing.

3.   Purpose of the anointing is to remove burdens and destroy yokes.

D.   D. UNDERSTANDING HIS PERSON V.27

1.   Son of God - Martha knew He was God

2.   Most people serve a little God.

3.   [Col 2:15 NASB95] 15 When He had disarmed the rulers and authorities, He made a public display of them, having triumphed over them through Him.

4.   Jesus paraded the devil.

CONCLUSION:

•   • Even Now faith based on

1.   Understanding His passion

2.   Understanding His position - Lord

3.   Understanding His purpose - Christ

4.   Understanding His person - Son of God

21 DAYS OF HEALING
PASTOR JOHN CARMICHAEL
SESSION 21
MESSAGE TITLE: HEALING IN DEMONSTRATION

[1Co 2:4 NASB95] 4 and my message and my preaching were not in persuasive words of wisdom, but in demonstration of the Spirit and of power,

INTRODUCTION:

- The Gospel was never intended to become just a philosophy.
- It was never just about the spiritual. It affects the corporeal (touchable)
- Mark 16:15-20 - What signs...these signs.

Interrogative: What do we need to know about divine healing?

Transitional: Here are six important areas of understanding we need to know about divine healing.

BODY:

I.   Method

A.   NATURAL

1. [1Ti 5:23 NASB95] 23 No longer drink water [exclusively,] but use a little wine for the sake of your stomach and your frequent ailments.

2. [2Ki 20:7 NASB95] 7 Then Isaiah said, "Take a cake of figs." And they took and laid [it] on the boil, and he recovered.

B.   SUPERNATURAL - NUMEROUS REFERENCES - SPIRITUAL LAWS MUST BE APPLIED.

C.   [PRO 4:20-22 NASB95] 20 MY SON, GIVE ATTENTION TO MY WORDS; INCLINE YOUR EAR TO MY SAYINGS. 21 DO NOT LET THEM DEPART FROM YOUR SIGHT; KEEP THEM IN THE MIDST OF YOUR HEART. 22 FOR THEY ARE LIFE TO THOSE WHO FIND THEM AND HEALTH TO ALL THEIR BODY.

II. Responsibility

A.   TAKE CARE OF THE TEMPLE - [1CO 6:19 NASB95] 19 OR DO YOU NOT KNOW THAT YOUR BODY IS A TEMPLE OF THE HOLY SPIRIT WHO IS IN YOU, WHOM YOU HAVE FROM GOD, AND THAT YOU ARE NOT YOUR OWN?

B.   TAKE CARE OF OTHERS - MARK 16:18 - JUST AS WE ARE COMMANDED TO PREACH THE GOSPEL, WE ARE COMMANDED TO LAY HANDS ON THE SICK. [MAR 16:18 NASB95] 18 THEY WILL PICK UP SERPENTS, AND IF THEY DRINK ANY DEADLY [POISON,] IT WILL NOT HURT THEM; THEY WILL LAY HANDS ON THE SICK, AND THEY WILL RECOVER."

C.   HEBREWS 6:1-2 - PROMOTION IN MINISTRY, RELEASING OF MIRACLES [HEB 6:1-2 NASB95] 1 THEREFORE LEAVING THE ELEMENTARY TEACHING ABOUT THE CHRIST, LET US PRESS ON TO MATURITY, NOT LAYING AGAIN A FOUNDATION OF REPENTANCE FROM DEAD WORKS AND OF FAITH TOWARD GOD, 2 OF INSTRUC-

TION ABOUT WASHINGS AND LAYING ON OF HANDS, AND THE RES-
URRECTION OF THE DEAD AND ETERNAL JUDGMENT.

III. Progression

A.   SOME INSTANT - WOMAN WITH THE ISSUE OF BLOOD

B.   SOME PROGRESSIVE

1. [Luk 17:14 NASB95] 14 When He saw them, He said to them, "Go and show yourselves to the priests." And as they were going, they were cleansed.

2. [Mar 8:23-25 NASB95] 23 Taking the blind man by the hand, He brought him out of the village; and after spitting on his eyes and laying His hands on him, He asked him, "Do you see anything?" 24 And he looked up and said, "I see men, for I see [them] like trees, walking around." 25 Then again He laid His hands on his eyes; and he looked intently and was restored, and [began] to see everything clearly.

IV. Manifestation

A.   GIFTS OF HEALINGS - AS THE SPIRIT WILLS - [1CO
12:7-11 NASB95] 7 BUT TO EACH ONE IS GIVEN THE MANIFES-
TATION OF THE SPIRIT FOR THE COMMON GOOD. 8 FOR TO ONE
IS GIVEN THE WORD OF WISDOM THROUGH THE SPIRIT, AND TO
ANOTHER THE WORD OF KNOWLEDGE ACCORDING TO THE SAME
SPIRIT; 9 TO ANOTHER FAITH BY THE SAME SPIRIT, AND TO ANOTH-
ER GIFTS OF HEALING BY THE ONE SPIRIT, 10 AND TO ANOTHER
THE EFFECTING OF MIRACLES, AND TO ANOTHER PROPHECY, AND
TO ANOTHER THE DISTINGUISHING OF SPIRITS, TO ANOTHER [VARI-

OUS] KINDS OF TONGUES, AND TO ANOTHER THE INTERPRETATION OF TONGUES. 11 BUT ONE AND THE SAME SPIRIT WORKS ALL THESE THINGS, DISTRIBUTING TO EACH ONE INDIVIDUALLY JUST AS HE WILLS.

B.   LIVE BY FAITH - AS WE RESPOND.

1.   [Heb 10:36-38 NASB95] 36 For you have need of endurance, so that when you have done the will of God, you may receive what was promised. 37 FOR YET IN A VERY LITTLE WHILE, HE WHO IS COMING WILL COME, AND WILL NOT DELAY. 38 BUT MY RIGHTEOUS ONE SHALL LIVE BY FAITH; AND IF HE SHRINKS BACK, MY SOUL HAS NO PLEASURE IN HIM.

2.   [Mar 11:23-24 NASB95] 23 "Truly I say to you, whoever says to this mountain, 'Be taken up and cast into the sea,' and does not doubt in his heart, but believes that what he says is going to happen, it will be [granted] him. 24 "Therefore I say to you, all things for which you pray and ask, believe that you have received them, and they will be [granted] you.

V.   Authority -

[Luk 5:24 NASB95] 24 "But, so that you may know that the Son of Man has authority on earth to forgive sins," He said to the paralytic "I say to you, get up, and pick up your stretcher and go home."

A.   IF HE CAN FORGIVE SIN.

B.   HE CAN HEAL SICKNESS.

VI. Atonement - Isaiah 53:4 & Matthew 8:16-17; Psalm 103; James 5:14-15

A. HE PAID FOR YOUR SIN.

B. HE PAID FOR YOUR HEALING.

C. [ISA 53:4 NASB95] 4 SURELY OUR GRIEFS HE HIMSELF BORE, AND OUR SORROWS HE CARRIED; YET WE OURSELVES ESTEEMED HIM STRICKEN, SMITTEN OF GOD, AND AFFLICTED.

D. [MAT 8:16-17 NASB95] 16 WHEN EVENING CAME, THEY BROUGHT TO HIM MANY WHO WERE DEMON-POSSESSED; AND HE CAST OUT THE SPIRITS WITH A WORD, AND HEALED ALL WHO WERE ILL. 17 [THIS WAS] TO FULFILL WHAT WAS SPOKEN THROUGH ISAIAH THE PROPHET: "HE HIMSELF TOOK OUR INFIRMITIES AND CARRIED AWAY OUR DISEASES."

E. [PSA 103:3 NASB95] 3 WHO PARDONS ALL YOUR INIQUITIES, WHO HEALS ALL YOUR DISEASES;

F. [JAS 5:14-15 NASB95] 14 IS ANYONE AMONG YOU SICK? [THEN] HE MUST CALL FOR THE ELDERS OF THE CHURCH AND THEY ARE TO PRAY OVER HIM, ANOINTING HIM WITH OIL IN THE NAME OF THE LORD; 15 AND THE PRAYER OFFERED IN FAITH WILL RESTORE THE ONE WHO IS SICK, AND THE LORD WILL RAISE HIM UP, AND IF HE HAS COMMITTED SINS, THEY WILL BE FORGIVEN HIM.

CONCLUSION:

- Allow God to demonstrate His healing power in your life.

CHAPTER 9

Healing Scriptures

Unless otherwise indicated, all Bible references in this list are to the New American Standard Bible (NASB) (La Habra, CA: The Lockman Foundation, 1995).

[Exo 15:26 NASB95] 26 And He said, "If you will give earnest heed to the voice of the LORD your God, and do what is right in His sight, and give ear to His commandments, and keep all His statutes, I will put none of the diseases on you which I have put on the Egyptians; for I, the LORD, am your healer."

[Exo 23:25-26 NASB95] 25 "But you shall serve the LORD your God, and He will bless your bread and your water; and I will remove sickness from your midst. 26 "There shall be no one miscarrying or barren in your land; I will fulfill the number of your days.

[Deu 7:14-15 NASB95] 14 "You shall be blessed above all peoples; there will be no male or female barren among you or among your cattle. 15 "The LORD will remove from you all sickness; and He will not put on you any of the harmful diseases of Egypt which you have known, but He will lay them on all who hate you.

[Deu 30:19-20 NASB95] 19 "I call heaven and earth to witness against you today, that I have set before you life and death, the blessing and the curse. So choose life in order that you may live, you and your descendants, 20 by loving the LORD your God, by obeying His voice, and by holding fast to Him; for this is your life and the length of your days, that you may live in the land which the LORD swore to your fathers, to Abraham, Isaac, and Jacob, to give them."

[1Ki 8:56 NASB95] 56 "Blessed be the LORD, who has given rest to His people Israel, according to all that He promised; not one word has failed of all His good promise, which He promised through Moses His servant.

[Psa 91:9-10, 14-16 NASB95] 9 For you have made the LORD, my refuge, [Even] the Most High, your dwelling place. 10 No evil will befall you, Nor will any plague come near your tent. ... 14 "Because he has loved Me, therefore I will deliver him; I will set him [securely] on high, because he has known My name. 15 "He will call upon Me, and I will answer him; I will be with him in trouble; I will rescue him and honor him. 16 "With a long life I will satisfy him And let him see My salvation."

[Psa 103:1-5 NASB95] 1 [A Psalm] of David. Bless the LORD, O my soul, And all that is within me, [bless] His holy name. 2 Bless the LORD, O my soul, And forget none of His benefits; 3 Who pardons all your iniquities, Who heals all your diseases; 4 Who redeems your life from the pit, Who crowns you with lovingkindness and compassion; 5 Who satisfies your years with good things, [So that] your youth is renewed like the eagle.

[Psa 107:17, 19-21 NASB95] 17 Fools, because of their rebellious way, And because of their iniquities, were afflicted. ... 19 Then they cried out to the LORD in their trouble; He saved them out of their distresses. 20 He sent His word and healed them, And delivered [them] from their destructions. 21 Let them give thanks to the LORD for His lovingkindness, And for His wonders to the sons of men!

[Psa 118:17 NASB95] 17 I will not die, but live, And tell of the works of the LORD.

[Pro 4:20-24 NASB95] 20 My son, give attention to my words; Incline your ear to my sayings. 21 Do not let them depart from your sight; Keep them in the midst of your heart. 22 For they are life to those who find them And health to all their body. 23 Watch over your heart with all diligence, For from it [flow] the springs of life. 24 Put away from you a deceitful mouth And put devious speech far from you.

[Isa 41:10 NASB95] 10 'Do not fear, for I am with you; Do not anxiously look about you, for I am your God. I will strengthen you, surely I will help you, Surely I will uphold you with My righteous right hand.'

[Isa 53:4-5 NASB95] 4 Surely our griefs He Himself bore, And our sorrows He carried; Yet we ourselves esteemed Him stricken, Smitten of God, and afflicted. 5 But He was pierced through for our transgressions, He was crushed for our iniquities; The chastening for our well-being [fell] upon Him, And by His scourging we are healed.

[Jer 1:12 NASB95] 12 Then the LORD said to me, "You have seen well, for I am watching over My word to perform it."

[Jer 17:14 NASB95] 14 Heal me, O LORD, and I will be healed; Save me and I will be saved, For You are my praise.

[Jer 30:17 NASB95] 17 'For I will restore you to health And I will heal you of your wounds,' declares the LORD, 'Because they have called you an outcast, saying: "It is Zion; no one cares for her."'

[Joe 3:10 NASB95] 10 Beat your plowshares into swords And your pruning hooks into spears; Let the weak say, "I am a mighty man."

[Nah 1:9 NASB95] 9 Whatever you devise against the LORD, He will make a complete end of it. Distress will not rise up twice.

[Mat 4:23 NASB95] 23 Jesus was going throughout all Galilee, teaching in their synagogues, and proclaiming the gospel of the kingdom, and healing every kind of disease and every kind of sickness among the people.

[Mat 8:2-3 NASB95] 2 And a leper came to Him and bowed down before Him, and said, "Lord, if You are willing, You can make me clean." 3 Jesus stretched out His hand and touched him, saying, "I am willing; be cleansed." And immediately his leprosy was cleansed.

[Mat 8:16-17 NASB95] 16 When evening came, they brought to Him many who were demon-possessed; and He cast out the spirits with a word, and healed all who were ill. 17 [This was] to fulfill what was spoken through Isaiah the prophet: "HE HIMSELF TOOK OUR INFIRMITIES AND CARRIED AWAY OUR DISEASES."

[Mat 9:35 NASB95] 35 Jesus was going through all the cities and villages, teaching in their synagogues and proclaiming the gospel of the kingdom, and healing every kind of disease and every kind of sickness.

[Mat 10:1, 7-8 NASB95] 1 Jesus summoned His twelve disciples and gave them authority over unclean spirits, to cast them out, and to heal every kind of disease and every kind of sickness. ... 7 "And as you go, preach, saying, 'The kingdom of heaven is at hand.' 8 "Heal [the] sick, raise [the] dead, cleanse [the] lepers, cast out demons. Freely you received, freely give.

[Mat 15:30-31 NASB95] 30 And large crowds came to Him, bringing with them [those who were] lame, crippled, blind, mute, and many others, and they laid them down at His feet; and He healed them. 31 So the crowd marveled as they saw the mute speaking, the crippled restored, and the lame walking, and the blind seeing; and they glorified the God of Israel.

[Mat 18:18-19 NASB95] 18 "Truly I say to you, whatever you bind on earth shall have been bound in heaven; and whatever you loose on earth shall have been loosed in heaven. 19 "Again I say to you, that if two of you agree on earth about anything that they may ask, it shall be done for them by My Father who is in heaven.

[Mat 21:21-22 NASB95] 21 And Jesus answered and said to them, "Truly I say to you, if you have faith and do not doubt, you will not only do what was done to the fig tree, but even if you say to this mountain, 'Be taken up and cast into the sea,' it will happen. 22 "And all things you ask in prayer, believing, you will receive."

[Mar 9:23 NASB95] 23 And Jesus said to him, " 'If You can?' All things are possible to him who believes."

[Mar 10:27 NASB95] 27 Looking at them, Jesus said, "With people it is impossible, but not with God; for all things are possible with God."

[Mar 11:22-24 NASB95] 22 And Jesus answered saying to them, "Have faith in God. 23 "Truly I say to you, whoever says to this mountain,

'Be taken up and cast into the sea,' and does not doubt in his heart, but believes that what he says is going to happen, it will be [granted] him. 24 "Therefore I say to you, all things for which you pray and ask, believe that you have received them, and they will be [granted] you.

[Mar 16:14-18 NASB95] 14 Afterward He appeared to the eleven themselves as they were reclining [at the table;] and He reproached them for their unbelief and hardness of heart, because they had not believed those who had seen Him after He had risen. 15 And He said to them, "Go into all the world and preach the gospel to all creation. 16 "He who has believed and has been baptized shall be saved; but he who has disbelieved shall be condemned. 17 "These signs will accompany those who have believed: in My name they will cast out demons, they will speak with new tongues; 18 they will pick up serpents, and if they drink any deadly [poison,] it will not hurt them; they will lay hands on the sick, and they will recover."

[Luk 6:19 NASB95] 19 And all the people were trying to touch Him, for power was coming from Him and healing [them] all.

[Luk 9:2 NASB95] 2 And He sent them out to proclaim the kingdom of God and to perform healing.

[Luk 13:16 NASB95] 16 "And this woman, a daughter of Abraham as she is, whom Satan has bound for eighteen long years, should she not have been released from this bond on the Sabbath day?"

[Act 5:16 NASB95] 16 Also the people from the cities in the vicinity of Jerusalem were coming together, bringing people who were sick or afflicted with unclean spirits, and they were all being healed.

[Act 10:38 NASB95] 38 "[You know of] Jesus of Nazareth, how God anointed Him with the Holy Spirit and with power, and [how] He went about doing good and healing all who were oppressed by the devil, for God was with Him.

[Rom 4:16-21 NASB95] 16 For this reason [it is] by faith, in order that [it may be] in accordance with grace, so that the promise will be guaranteed to all the descendants, not only to those who are of the Law, but also to those who are of the faith of Abraham, who is the father of us all, 17 (as it is written, "A FATHER OF MANY NATIONS HAVE I MADE YOU") in the presence of Him whom he believed, [even] God, who gives life to the dead and calls into being that which does not exist. 18 In hope against hope he believed, so that he might become a father of many nations according to that which had been spoken, "SO SHALL YOUR DESCENDANTS BE." 19 Without becoming weak in faith he contemplated his own body, now as good as dead since he was about a hundred years old, and the deadness of Sarah's womb; 20 yet, with respect to the promise of God, he did not waver in unbelief but grew strong in faith, giving glory to God, 21 and being fully assured that what God had promised, He was able also to perform.

[Rom 8:2, 11 NASB95] 2 For the law of the Spirit of life in Christ Jesus has set you free from the law of sin and of death. ... 11 But if the Spirit of Him who raised Jesus from the dead dwells in you, He who raised Christ Jesus from the dead will also give life to your mortal bodies through His Spirit who dwells in you.

[Rom 10:17 NASB95] 17 So faith [comes] from hearing, and hearing by the word of Christ.

[2Co 4:18 NASB95] 18 while we look not at the things which are seen, but at the things which are not seen; for the things which are seen are temporal, but the things which are not seen are eternal.

[2Co 10:3-5 NASB95] 3 For though we walk in the flesh, we do not war according to the flesh, 4 for the weapons of our warfare are not of the flesh, but divinely powerful for the destruction of fortresses. 5 [We are] destroying speculations and every lofty thing raised up against the knowledge of God, and [we are] taking every thought captive to the obedience of Christ,

[Gal 3:13-14, 29 NASB95] 13 Christ redeemed us from the curse of the Law, having become a curse for us for it is written, "CURSED IS EVERYONE WHO HANGS ON A TREE" 14 in order that in Christ Jesus the blessing of Abraham might come to the Gentiles, so that we would receive the promise of the Spirit through faith. ... 29 And if you belong to Christ, then you are Abraham's descendants, heirs according to promise.

[Eph 6:10-17 NASB95] 10 Finally, be strong in the Lord and in the strength of His might. 11 Put on the full armor of God, so that you will be able to stand firm against the schemes of the devil. 12 For our struggle is not against flesh and blood, but against the rulers, against the powers, against the world forces of this darkness, against the spiritual [forces] of wickedness in the heavenly [places.] 13 Therefore, take up the full armor of God, so that you will be able to resist in the evil day, and having done everything, to stand firm. 14 Stand firm therefore, HAVING GIRDED YOUR LOINS WITH TRUTH, and HAVING PUT ON THE BREASTPLATE OF RIGHTEOUSNESS, 15 and having shod YOUR FEET WITH THE PREPARATION OF THE GOSPEL OF PEACE; 16 in addition to all, taking up the shield of faith with which you will be able to extinguish all the flaming arrows of the evil [one.] 17 And take THE HELMET OF SALVATION, and the sword of the Spirit, which is the word of God.

[Phl 4:6-9 NASB95] 6 Be anxious for nothing, but in everything by prayer and supplication with thanksgiving let your requests be made known to God. 7 And the peace of God, which surpasses all comprehension, will guard your hearts and your minds in Christ Jesus. 8 Finally, brethren, whatever is true, whatever is honorable, whatever is right, whatever is pure, whatever is lovely, whatever is of good repute, if there is any excellence and if anything worthy of praise, dwell on these things. 9 The things you have learned and received and heard and seen in me, practice these things, and the God of peace will be with you.

[2Ti 1:7 NASB95] 7 For God has not given us a spirit of timidity, but of power and love and discipline.

[Heb 10:23 NASB95] 23 Let us hold fast the confession of our hope without wavering, for He who promised is faithful;

[Heb 10:35-36 NASB95] 35 Therefore, do not throw away your confidence, which has a great reward. 36 For you have need of endurance, so that when you have done the will of God, you may receive what was promised.

[Heb 11:11 NASB95] 11 By faith even Sarah herself received ability to conceive, even beyond the proper time of life, since she considered Him faithful who had promised.

[Heb 13:8 NASB95] 8 Jesus Christ [is] the same yesterday and today and forever.

[Jas 4:7 NASB95] 7 Submit therefore to God. Resist the devil and he will flee from you.

[Jas 5:14-16 NASB95] 14 Is anyone among you sick? [Then] he must call for the elders of the church and they are to pray over him, anointing him with oil in the name of the Lord; 15 and the prayer offered in faith will restore the one who is sick, and the Lord will raise him up, and if he has committed sins, they will be forgiven him. 16 Therefore, confess your sins to one another, and pray for one another so that you may be healed. The effective prayer of a righteous man can accomplish much.

[1Pe 2:24 NASB95] 24 and He Himself bore our sins in His body on the cross, so that we might die to sin and live to righteousness; for by His wounds you were healed.

[1Jo 3:21-22 NASB95] 21 Beloved, if our heart does not condemn us, we have confidence before God; 22 and whatever we ask we receive from Him, because we keep His commandments and do the things that are pleasing in His sight.

[1Jo 5:14-15 NASB95] 14 This is the confidence which we have before Him, that, if we ask anything according to His will, He hears us. 15 And if we know that He hears us [in] whatever we ask, we know that we have the requests which we have asked from Him.

[3Jo 1:2 NASB95] 2 Beloved, I pray that in all respects you may prosper and be in good health, just as your soul prospers.

[Rev 12:11 NASB95] 11 "And they overcame him because of the blood of the Lamb and because of the word of their testimony, and they did not love their life even when faced with death.

BIBLIOGRAPHY

Books

Achtemeier, Paul J. *Romans.* Interpretation, a Bible Commentary for Teaching and Preaching. Atlanta: Westminster John Knox Press, 1985.

Bauer, Walter, and Frederick W. Danker. "Διδάσκω." Essay. In *A Greek-English Lexicon of the New Testament and Other Early Christian Literature*. Chicago, Il: Univ. of Chicago Press, 2000.

"ἴασις." Essay. In *A Greek-English Lexicon of the New Testament and Other Early Christian Literature*. Chicago, Il: Univ. of Chicago Press, 2000.

"Θεραπεύω." Essay. In *A Greek-English Lexicon of the New Testament and Other Early Christian Literature*, 453. Chicago, Il: Univ. of Chicago Press, 2000.

"Κηρύσσω." Essay. In *A Greek-English Lexicon of the New Testament and Other Early Christian Literature*, 543–544. Chicago, Il: Univ. of Chicago Press, 2000.

"Μαλακία." Essay. In *A Greek-English Lexicon of the New Testament and Other Early Christian Literature*. Chicago, Il: Univ. of Chicago Press, 2000.

"Νόσος." Essay. In *A Greek-English Lexicon of the New Testament and Other Early Christian Literature*. Chicago, Il: Univ. of Chicago Press, 2000.

Blue, Ken. Authority to Heal. Downers Grove, Ill.: InterVarsity Press. 1987.

Burgess, Stanley M. Encyclopedia of Pentecostal and Charismatic Christianity. New York: Taylor & Francis Group, 2006. Clark, Randy. There is More. Chosen: Bloomington, Minnesota, 2013.

Collins, Robert Don. "Healing through Story: Exploring the Use of Storytelling Preaching as a Means for Healing a Congregation." PhD diss., Mercer University, Macon, GA, 2018. ProQuest Dissertations & Theses Global.

Cox, Richard H. Rewiring Your Preaching. Downers Grove: Intervarsity Press, 2012.

Ervin, Howard. Healing: Sign of the Kingdom. Peabody: Hendrickson Publishers, 2002.

Friesen, Ivan. *Isaiah: Believers Church Bible Commentary*. Believers Church Bible Commentary. Scottdale, Pa: Herald Press, 2009.

Grizzle, Trevor. Church Aflame: An Exposition of Acts 1–12. Cleveland, TN: Pathway Press, 2000.

Hagin, Kenneth E. Hear and Be Healed. Tulsa, OK: Rhema Bible Church, 1987.

Hall, Newman. Atonement: The Fundamental Fact of Christianity. New York: F. H. Revell, 1893.

Harrell Jr., David, Edwin. Oral Roberts: An American Life. Bloomington: Indiana Press, 1985.

Hart, Colin. Receive Healing, Trans., Kwang Ho Lee, Seoul: Christian Literature Society, 1988.

Horton, Stanley, Menzies, William W. *Bible Doctrines: A Pentecostal Perspective*. Logion Press, 2015.

Horton, Stanley. *What the Bible Says About the Holy Spirit?*. Springfield, MO: Gospel Publishing House, 2005.

Hunter, Joan. *Power to Heal*. New Kensington, PA: Whitaker House, 2009.

Hyatt, Eddie L. *2000 Years of Charismatic Christianity*. Lake Mary: Charisma House, 2015.

I. Howard Marshall, *Luke*, ed. D. A Carson, et al., New Bible Commentary: 21st Century Edition. Downers Grove: InterVarsity Press, 1994.

Johnson, Luke Timothy. Hebrews: A Commentary. Louisville: Presbyterian Publishing Corporation, 2006.

Kennedy, Sandra. The Simplicity of Healing: A Practical Guide to Releasing the Miracle Power of God's Word. Charlotte, NC: It's Supernatural & Messianic Vision, Inc., 2017.

Kim, Lee. "Increasing Faith through Preaching Sermons on Worship in Sunday Morning Sermons." Doctor of Ministry, Oral Roberts University, Tulsa, OK, 2008. ProQuest Dissertations & Theses Global.

Kim, Yong. "Increasing Faith through Teaching About Divine Healing." Doctor of Ministry, Oral Roberts University, Tulsa, OK, 2006. ProQuest Dissertations & Theses Global.

King, Paul. "A Practical-Theological Investigation Of Nineteenth and Twentieth Century 'Faith Theologies'." Doctor of Theology, University of South Africa, 2001. ProQuest Dissertations & Theses Global.

Kydd, Ronald A. N. Healing through the Centuries: Models for Understanding. Peabody, MA: Hendrickson, 1998.

Lake, John G. Divine Healing: A Gift from God. Orlando, FL: GodSounds, Inc. 2016.

. Letter to Mrs. Carrie Judd Montgomery. Alameda, CO: Beulah Heights, April 22, 1911.

Lapin, Hayim. "Medicine and Healing." Vol. 4 in Anchor Bible Dictionary. Edited by David Noel Freedman. New York: Doubleday, 1992.

. "Preaching." Vol. 5 in Anchor Bible Dictionary. Edited by David Noel Freedman. New York: Doubleday, 1992.

. "Sickness." Vol. 6 in Anchor Bible Dictionary. Edited by David Noel Freedman. New York: Doubleday, 1992.

Levin, Jeff, and Meador, Keith. *Healing to All Their Flesh: Jewish and Christian Perspectives on Spirituality, Theology, and Health.* West Conshohocken, Pa: Templeton Press, 2012.

Longenecker, Richard N. *The Epistle to the Romans: A Commentary on the Greek Text.* Grand Rapids: William B. Eerdmans Publishing Company, 2016.

Mathew, Thomson K. *Spirit-Led Ministry in the Twenty-First: Spirit-Empowered Preaching, Teaching, Healing, and Leadership.* WestBow Press, 2017.

McKnight, Scot. "Extending Jesus." In Devotions on the Greek New Testament: 52 Reflections to Inspire & Instruct, edited by J. Scott Duvall, and Verlyn D. Verbrugge. Grand Rapids, MI: Zondervan, 2012.

Mitch, Curtis, and Edward Sri. *The Gospel of Matthew*. Baker Academic, 2010.

New American Standard Bible. La Habra, CA: The Lockman Foundation, 1995.

Porterfield, Amanda. Healing in the History of Christianity. Oxford: Oxford Press, 2005.

Reichenbach, Bruce R. "Healing View." In The Nature of the Atonement: Four Views. Spectrum Multiview Book Series, edited by James K. Beilby and Paul R. Eddy. 117–155. Downers Grove, IL: IVP Academic, 2006.

Rodgers, Robert Waymon. "A Study of the Relationship between Biblical Fasting and Financial Prosperity." D.Min. ARP, Oral Roberts University, Tulsa, OK, 2002. ProQuest Dissertations & Theses Global.

Schaff, Philip. *History of the Christian Church, Volume V: The Middle Ages, A.D. 1049–1294*. Grand Rapids: William B. Eerdmans Publishing Company, 1960.

Schmid, Deborah. "Healing in the Atonement of Isaiah 52:13–53:6." Masters Thesis, Graduate School of Theology and Ministry, Oral Roberts University, 2013. ProQuest Dissertations & Theses Global.

Talbert, Charles H. *Matthew*. Baker Academic, 2010.

Ward, David. "Our Lives as Well: Teaching Preaching as a Formative Christian Practice." PhD diss., Princeton Theological Seminary, Princeton, New Jersey, 2012). ProQuest Dissertations & Theses Global.

Warrington, Keith. "The Teaching and Praxis Concerning Supernatural Healing of British Pentecostals, of John Wimber and Kenneth Hagin in the Light of an Analysis of the Healing Ministry of Jesus as Recorded in the Gospels." Doctor of Philosophy, Kings College, London, 1999. ProQuest Dissertations & Theses Global.

Wommack, Andrew. *You've Already Got It! So Quit Trying to Get It.* Tulsa, OK: Harrison House Publishers, 2006.

Periodicals

Adamo, David T. "'I Am the LORD Your Healer' Exodus 15:26 (רָאפְרהוהיינא): Healing in the Old Testament and the African (Yoruba) Context." In *Die Skriflig* 55, no. 1 (May 1, 2021): 1–8. doi:10.4102/ids. v55i1.2689.

Andrade, Chittaranjan, and Rajiv Radhakrishnan. "Prayer and Healing: A Medical and Scientific Perspective on Randomized Controlled Trials." *Indian Journal of Psychiatry* 51, no. 4 (2009): 247–253. https://www.ncbi. nlm.nih.gov/pmc/articles/PMC2802370/.

Augustson, Michael Keith. "Teach, Preach, and Heal: A Series of Prescriptions for the Church on Health and Health-Care Reform." The Covenant Quarterly 64, no. 1–3 (February 2006): 304–21.

Bradley, James, "Miracles and Martyrdom in the Early Church: Some Theological and Ethical Implications." *Pneuma* 13, no. 1 (Spr 1991): 65–81.

Brown, Candy. "Jesus the Healer." *Christian History*, no. 142 (January 1, 2022): 8–11.

Bukhari, Amal A., Yoon S. Park, Omayma A. Hamed, and Ara S. Tekian. "Cultural Influence on Generational Gaps: A Case for Medical Education in the Gulf Region." Saudi Medical Journal 40, no. 6 (2019): 601–9. https://doi.org/10.15537/smj.2019.6.23863.

Culpepper, R Alan. "Jesus as Healer in the Gospel of Matthew, Part II: Jesus as Healer in Matthew 8–9." In Die Skriflig 50, no. 1 (2016): 1–9. doi:10.4102/ids.v50i1.2116.

Derickson, Gary W. "The Cessation of Healing Miracles in Paul's Ministry." Bibliotheca Sacra 155, no. 619 (July 1998): 299–315.

Dessauer, Phil. "God Heals, I Don't." Coronet Magazine. (October 1955): 52–61.

Harmon, Cedric. "Former Baptist Woman Pioneers Charismatic Healing Center in Georgia." *Charisma Magazine*. (June 30, 2000). https://mycharisma.com/charisma-archive/former-baptist-woman-pioneers-charismatic-healing-center-in-georgia/#:~:text=It%20wasn't%20until%20Sandra,where%20miracles%20are%20the%20norm.

Hart, Richard. "Preaching and Healing: Best Form of Healing Is to Preach with a Spirit of Joy." The Priest 72, no. 8 (August 2016): 20.

Heim, Knut Martin. Poetic Imagination in Proverbs: Variant Repetitions and the Nature of Poetry, Pennsylvania State University Press, 2012.

Hejzlar, Pavel. "John Calvin and the Cessation of Miraculous Healing." Communio Viatorum 49, no. 1 (2007): 31–77.

Hill, Judith L. "Health, Sickness, and Healing in the New Testament: A Brief Theology." Africa Journal of Evangelical Theology 27, no. 1 (2008): 151–95.

Holm, Randall. "Healing in Search of Atonement with a Little Help from James K.A. Smith." Journal of Pentecostal Theology 23, no. 1 (April 2014): 50–67. doi:10.1163/17455251-02301007.

Hwang, Sunwoo. "Participation in Christ's Suffering in 1 Peter 4:1–6." 성경과 신학 82 (2017): 133–50.

Jones, Richard S. 2019. "The Healing Power of Christ: Scripture Shows the Importance of Faith to Those Who Are Ill." *The Priest* 75 (2): 40–45.

Kingsbury, Jack Dean. "Observations on the 'Miracle Chapters' of Matthew 8–9." The Catholic Biblical Quarterly 40, no. 4 (October 1978): 559–73.

Moo, Douglas. "Divine Healing in the Health and Wealth Gospel." Trinity Journal 9, no. 2 (Fall 1988): 191–209.

Nihinlola, Emiola. "'By His Wounds, We Are Healed;' a Theological Examination of the Nature of Healing in the Atonement." Ogbomosa Journal of Theology XVII (2013): 19–26.

Onylnah, Opoku. "God's Grace, Healing, and Suffering." International Review of Mission 95, no. 377 (January 4, 2006): 117–27.

Poirier, John C. "Narrative Theology and Pentecostal Commitments." Journal of Pentecostal Theology 16, no. 2 (April 2008): 69–85. doi:10.1163/174552508X294206

Prudlo, Donald. "Speaking with the Saints." *Christian History,* no. 142 (January 1, 2022): 16–18.

Rittgers, Ronald. "We Have Prayed Three People to Life." *Christian History*, no. 142 (January 1, 2022): 19–22.

Spaces, Crosslife. "A Christian Woman's Worth – She Hears God." *Fifty Percent Perspective -Women's Best.* Last modified July 16, 2014. Accessed March 14, 2021. https://kingdomofgodaughter.wordpress.com/2013/11/01/random-hearing-another-womans-worth-a-woman-who-hears-god/.

Synan, Vinson. "A Healer in the House? A Historical Perspective on Healing in the Pentecostal/Charismatic Tradition." Asian Journal of Pentecostal Studies 3, no. 2 (July 2000): 189.

Trask, Thomas. "Defining Truths Of The Assemblies Of God: Divine Healing." Enrichment Q3 (2007): 1.

Werntz, Myles. "The Fellowship of Suffering: Reading Philippians with Stanley Hauerwas." *Review & Expositor* 112, no. 1 (February 2015): 144–50. doi:10.1177/0034637314564548.

Other Sources

Andrew Wommack Ministries. "Executive Management Staff - Andrew Wommack Ministries." Last modified 2021. https://www.awmi.net/about-us/management-staff/.

Baldwin, Wesley James. "The Centrality of Preaching in Christian Worship." PhD diss., Southwestern Baptist Theological Seminary, Fort Worth, TX, 2015. ProQuest Dissertations & Theses Global.

Bible Study Tools. "What Does the Bible Say about Meditation?" Accessed November 29, 2019. https://www.biblestudytools.com/bible-study/topical-studies/what-does-the-bible-say-about-meditation.html.

Blue Letter Bible. "G2392 - iasis - Strong's Greek Lexicon (NASB)." Accessed September 20, 2020. https://www.blueletterbible.org//lang/lexicon/lexicon. cfm?Strongs=G2392&t=NASB.

Census Bureau Quickfacts. "U.S. Census Bureau QuickFacts: Clark County, Indiana." Last modified 2022. https://www.census.gov/quickfacts/fact/table/clarkcounty indiana, IN/PST045221.

Cgiamericas.Org, "About Us." Last modified 2020. www.cgiamericas.org/cgiahome.

"Core Values." Last modified 2020. https://www.cgiamericas.org.

Cox, Jennifer. "A Re-Examination of Faith and Healing in the Gospels: Toward a Pentecostal Theology of Healing and Disability." *Cyberjournal*

for Pentecostal-Charismatic Research 24 (June 2017). http://www.pctii.org.
oralroberts.idm. oclc.org/cyberj/cyberj24/cox.html.

Data Census Gov. "ACS Demographic and Housing
Estimates 2020." Last modified 2022. https://data.
census.gov/table/ACSDP5Y2020.DP05?g=050XX00US1
8019_010XX00US&moe=false.&tid=ACSDP5Y2020.DP05

. "Selected Economic Characteristics 2020." Last modified 2022.
https://data. census.gov/table/ACSDP5Y2020.DP03?t=Income%20
and%20Poverty&g=050XX00US18019&tid=ACSDP5Y2020.DP03.

. "Selected Social Characteristics in the United States." Last modified
2022. https://data.census.gov/table/ACSDP5Y2020.DP02.

Harnack, Adolf von. The Mission and Expansion of Christianity in
the First Three Centuries. Grand Rapids, MI: Christian Classics Ethereal
Library, 1908.

Healing Rooms Ministries. "John G. Lake." Accessed March 14, 2021.
https://healingrooms.com/about/johnGLake/summary/.

. "Leadership." Accessed March 14, 2021. https://healingrooms.
com/about/leadership/.

Hofstede Insights. "Country Comparison - Hofstede Insights." Last
modified 2020. https://www.hofstede-insights.com/country-comparison/
the-usa.

"How to Start Healing Rooms: A Manual." Spokane, WA: International
Association of Healing Rooms. 2000.

Kenneth Hagin Ministries. "Hear and Be Healed." Accessed March 14, 2021. https://www.rhema.org/index.php?option=com_content&view=article&id=2574%3Ahear-and-be-healed&catid=259&Itemid=11.

JGLM. "John G. Lake." Accessed March 14, 2021. https://www.jglm.org/john-g-lake/.

Joan Hunter Ministries. "Joan Hunter." Accessed March 14, 2021. https://joanhunter.org/about-joan/.

Newadvent.Org. "Church Fathers: City Of God, Book XXII (St. Augustine)." Accessed June 15, 2018, https://www.newadvent.org/fathers/120122.htm.

Sandra Kennedy Ministries. "About." Accessed May 8, 2021. https://www.sandrakennedy.org/about/.

. "Healing Center." Admin. Last modified February 26, 2021. Accessed March 14, 2021. https://www.sandrakennedy.org/healing-center/.

The General Council of the Assemblies of God. "Assemblies of God (USA) Official Web Site | Divine Healing." Accessed June 10, 2022. https://ag.org/Beliefs/Our-Core-Doctrines/Divine-Healing.

DR. JOHN CARMICHAEL

www.ingramcontent.com/pod-product-compliance
Lightning Source LLC
Chambersburg PA
CBHW071720120626
46550CB00001B/316